MW00957661

TAKE IT BACK

Your Strength

Your Mindset

Your Finances

Nicole Henderson RN, BSN

Copyright © 2019 Unstoppable Nicole LLC

All rights reserved.

No part of this book can be reproduced in any form without the
written permission of the author and its publisher.

ISBN:9781083134158

DEDICATION

I'm dedicating this book to my daughter Blessing. Since her first day of life she reminded me of how powerful, focused and impactful I'm supposed to be! These past 3 years her strength, wisdom and love has awakened me. Her heart has stolen the hearts of many. Thank you to my two sons, my family and friends. With all the love in my heart, I say thank you to my village that has helped me with all 3 kids. You know who you are and there are too many of you to name.
How Blessed is that? I am grateful for all of you!

CONTENTS

Dedication

Acknowledgement

About the Author

ACKNOWLEDGMENTS

God/Jesus/Holy Spirit who is the head of my life
Kathy Kidd/ Kidd Marketing
Alvin Moore/Ambitious Motives Media
Whitney Moore/Whitmore Artistry
Kendra N. Jones (Book Cover)/Website
Editor: New Jersey Author, Raven Moore
Sharon Fant
Errika Lowe
Melanie Outlaw

CHAPTER 1
THE LITTLE PROJECT GIRL

It was the norm for crackheads to smoke in our stairway. I would always smell crack being burned when I entered the building. The smell of crack is so bad, it gives you an instant headache. This was my family's daily experience in the small three-bedroom, one-bath apartment we called home, on the fifteenth floor of the Carver Projects. The elevators were usually broken. So, we had to walk up fifteen flights of stairs while passing dope fiends shooting up crack into their veins in the stairwells. Stepping over crack vials and dirty needles was not the childhood my parents intended for us. I was born and raised in Manhattan - in New York City, New York - the city so nice they named it twice. But I grew up in Spanish Harlem. That was not so nice.

I graduated Wolfson Senior High School at 16 years old. Too young to enlist on my own, I begged my mother to sign the papers and joined the Army at age 17. I became the first person to graduate college on my Dad's side. I graduated with my bachelor's degree in Registered Nursing (RN), the first RN in my family. My nursing career flourished quickly. I was fortunate to start out as an Intensive Care Unit (ICU) nurse and, a year and a half later, switched focus and became a Labor & Delivery (L&D) nurse. This opportunity was significant because this unit did not usually recruit nurses without L&D experience. I was the first to be granted this opportunity and the youngest RN on staff. I love being an L&D nurse, and the service I provide to families. I've assisted in delivering babies in showers, elevators, parking lots, and, of course, labor rooms. I am now the highest paid nurse on my unit.

When I was 25-years old, and a single Mom of one kid (now of three), I bought my first house. I am thankful that I've never had to depend on a man financially. I consider myself a Perseverance Expert. I have helped single Moms get back on their feet by providing lodging and other support, while also being a single mother myself. I have taught teenaged Bible Study classes. I experienced great joy being able to see God from a teen's perspective, and to watch them take their walks out into life as adults. But what made me different from so many other children around me, growing up in a society that told us none of the above things could ever be possible?

I am the youngest of four kids. Mom was 18 when she had my brother, and two children followed before she had me. My Dad met my Mom when my siblings were aged three, one, and three months old. Mom is a city girl from New York and Dad a country boy from North Carolina.

Dad worked in the cotton fields in our very own twentieth century and he was paid three dollars for every 100 pounds of cotton. My grandmother pulled him out of school part-time when he was nine, to help support his younger sisters. This did not keep him from setting his sights on bigger things as he got older. Before leaving school completely, Dad picked cotton four times a week and only attended to school twice a week. As a result, he fell behind in class and they stuck him at the back of the room. Dad left school completely after the sixth grade.

"I felt so dumb! Wasn't 'til the third-grade I learned my A, B, Cs. This teacher saw I was struggling, so she started staying after class with me to catch me up," my Dad shared. "My grandmother and her sisters used to be slaves," Dad went on. "You wouldn't believe the stuff they went through," he would say.

My Dad begged his mother to move to New York with other family members already up there, but my grandmother did not like New York. So, when my father saved up enough money from picking cotton, he ran away to New York at age 14. He stayed with an aunt and uncle. Dad sent money back to help his Mom and his three younger sisters. My grandmother understood, but boy was she mad.

My Dad is the greatest man I've ever met. I have never heard him yell at Mommy or us. "He always worked hard to provide for us", my brother said. If it was not for my parents' insistence on making it through, it would have been harder for me to ignore the naysayers in society who believed I would not amount to anything.

I am a Daddy's girl, and I don't feel bad about it. My Mom expects so much of my sister and I, but coddles my brothers, no matter how old they get. My Dad is the true definition of a man. My oldest brother told me Dad worked two jobs my entire childhood into adulthood. He was always there for all of us, and all on his sixth-grade education. That is why the one thing I cannot tolerate is a man who does not work, and who has a whole bunch of excuses. But Mom also pushed us. She looked for other avenues to give us better exposures to other ways of life. For example, when I was five, she put me in "The Fresh Air Fund." This program allowed inner city youth to go stay with families in the suburbs. I know some would say "Five years old? That is really young to send a girl there." But, looking at my current environment, just know it was the greatest decision my mother ever made for me.

The Fresh Air Fund program placed me with the most amazing family—the Lafferty's. I still remember the first time we met. All the kids participating in the program had to meet at the Port Authority Terminal on 42nd Street in Manhattan. Then, we went to Penn Station on 34th Street and took the train to meet the families with whom we were placed. When I got off the train with my Fresh Air Fund counselor, my new family was waiting for me - Gail and Bob, the parents, and their little girl Jo, who was my age. I fearlessly left the counselor's side and joined my new family to go to my new home in good old Sea Cliff, New York. I was never a shy child. I made everyone I met my family.

Wow, did they have a beautiful house! The Lafferty's had a long, wide driveway that fit at least ten cars in length, that led up to the house. Everything was humongous. We entered through the basement, which was half the size of my family's apartment. To my surprise, they had a dog. I had never had a pet before, but there she was, beautiful Mona. She jumped all over me, trying to lick my face. I was not ready, because when she stood up on her hind legs, she was taller than me. However, it was love at first sight! From that moment on, that dog followed me everywhere like a faithful companion.

Leaving the basement, we walked upstairs onto the main level, into a big kitchen with an island—my first time seeing one. There was an impressively long dining table, which sat at the back of the kitchen. Walking across to their huge living room, I noticed they had a grand piano, on which later, I would have the honor to receive piano lessons. On the same floor, was the front door, which led out to a beautifully furnished porch, high up on the second level. Sitting out there was peaceful, unlike being on my small balcony in the New York City, listening to loud buses, trucks, and cars on busy Madison Ave.

To my extreme pleasure, there was more house to explore. We walked up another set of stairs to the level that housed the bedrooms. Yet another set of stairs led to a loft, which was a whole other apartment. It had a kitchen, bathroom, and open area. Altogether, this one house had four levels - a shock to my five-year-old eyes, especially coming from a three-bedroom, one bath apartment, where six people lived. To my amazement, only three of them lived in this huge house. That was just incredible to me.

My first night went great. I got to meet La La and Pop Pop, the parents of my host family, and the grandparents to Jo. They welcomed me with open arms. They became my bonus grandparents and, as such, Pop Pop became the only grandfather I ever knew. Pop Pop would always go outside and smoke his pipe. I used to think my new Grandpa smoked a pipe like the cartoon character, Popeye the Sailor Man. I loved spinach and I loved Popeye so, in my mind, I knew I was going to love Pop Pop.

I remember one episode of the Cosby Show, the father put his daughter Rudy and one of her friends on each of his knees and began to bounce them around like they were riding on a horse. Pop Pop did this to me and Jo, too.

"Pop Pop!!!! Ahhhhh!" Jo and I would scream and laugh while bouncing around on his lap like we were in a rodeo.

"Ohhhhhh!!!!" he would tease in his gruffy voice. He wore corduroy pants and he was always sharply dressed.

Everyone wanted to meet 'Nikki,' as I was called. Jo's best friend, Sarah, along with her Mom and Dad, Nancy and Larry, came over. They lived three houses down across the street. We had an amazing dinner and I felt very welcomed by everyone. I could not wait for all the adventures sure to come in Sea Cliff, New York.

The first morning, I woke up to Mona licking my face. This was something that I had only seen in the movies and so I was a bit freaked out. In my upbringing, we did not allow animals to lick us in our faces. "Mona is just happy to see you," Jo explained. We ate breakfast and afterwards, there were more pets to meet. First, I went to help feed our pet rabbits. "We have rabbits!" I was floored. Next I met the cats. This city girl went from no pets, to the equivalent of having a barnyard.

"Hey Nikki, we're going to the beach," Gail told me. Their house was a three-minute drive to the beach. We packed up the car with all our beach balls and other toys, then stopped by to get Sarah, Jo's best friend who lived down the street. Then off we went to the beach. The three of us climbed up into the lifeguard's chair. We were so little sitting there and it was so high up, but we did it anyway. Gail took a picture of us that I still have to this day.

I didn't have my guard up. I really felt I was in a safe place and was just enjoying being a kid, whereas in New York City you gotta have street smarts. Even if you are a kid in NYC, you must be on guard. I know that might sound crazy to some people, but it is just the environment. Over the next few days, we had a lot of sleepovers and I met Erica, Emily, and Lauren who were more of Jo's friends. We really got along just to be some young little kids hanging out with each other for the first time, and especially being from different backgrounds. That is the one thing that I loved about the innocence of youth. We did not look at color. We just created friendships whenever the opportunity came.

My Lafferty family was White and mostly all the people in Sea Cliff were White. This was back in the mid-80s. Even today, Sea Cliff is over 90% White. One morning Gail came to us to inform of us of the next adventure. "We're going to the yacht club", she said. I was thinking, 'I have no clue what a yacht club is, but I'm ready to find out.' At the yacht club, we walked past a snack bar grilling the most wonderful smelling food—hamburgers chicken breasts, and juicy hot dogs on the grill. I saw French Fries pulled fresh out the grease and I was ready to burn my tongue trying to pop them in my mouth and chew fast. It all smelled sooo good. There were nachos with hot, melted nacho cheese. I was already thinking about which drink and dessert I would pick. Ice cream? Potato chips? Juice or a vanilla milkshake? I wanna eat rather than learn how to swim, now. If you've ever met me, you would know that I am a foodie and I have always been for as long as I can remember being alive! There are kids that do not like to eat. However, that was never my problem. After passing the grill, I saw a humongous pool— another of the perks of being a member of the yacht club.

On this day, I also met another special lady - Jo's friend Erica's Mom. Up until this point, I had been in Sea Cliff for about ten days and it was almost time to go back to NYC. I was a little bit homesick, but I was also enjoying my time away. Erica's Mom had some African American in her, I could tell, and her skin was brown, although it was a few shades lighter than mine. "Finally, a person with some brown skin," I thought and became eagerly aware. I grew up in New York where I usually see all different races, but out there in Sea Cliff, that wasn't the case.

"Just jump in and I'll catch you," Erica's honey-skinned Mom said, as she motioned me toward the pool. I did not know how to swim, but I trusted her. I held my breath and jumped in.

Down I went into the water, and she pulled me right back up. First, she taught me how to hold my breath. She then taught me how to float, tread water, and a few other swimming techniques.

This was my first time in a pool, but I wasn't afraid. Ninety percent of my friends back home in NYC did not know how to swim and here I was, five-years old, learning how to swim. I sat on Erica's Mom's legs on the steps of the pool and we compared our skin complexions.

"You have beautiful skin!" she proclaimed. But, as a five-year-old, I did not catch the significance of her compliments.

I discovered the significance as I got older, when certain people in my life would express shame at the color of their skin. But, because of Erica's Mom, I did not have this problem. I knew from the age of five, that my skin was beautiful. That is why you must be careful of who is around your kids and what they speak over them. I am just thankful that Erica's Mom spoke positivity and self-love over me.

The first time we visited La La and Pop Pop at their house, I was happily surprised to see they had a pool with a slide. I was so excited. Although I knew I had just learned how to swim, I was not going to let that stop me. La La put on her swimsuit and got in the pool—waiting for me at the bottom of the slide. Down the slide I went—time and time again—and every time, La La was at the bottom of the slide ready to pull me up out the water. Pop Pop would tell us stories over hot chocolate. His stories were always long, elaborate, and vivid. I would hang onto his every word. Sometimes, drool would slide down the side of my mouth and I'd have to wipe it up quickly with the back of my hand because I had left my mouth open in anticipation for so long. I was transfixed just waiting for what never-before-seen image Pop Pop was going to plant into my mind. I lost sense of all space and time sitting there thinking, 'Is this what it feels like to have a Grandpa?'

Meanwhile, La La went back in to cook dinner and, boy, could she cook! Then, later that afternoon in the yard I spotted my first deer. "Bambie's in the front yard! Bambie's in the front yard! Look! Bambie's family is there, too!" I screamed happily.

Everyone just laughed because I was so amazed and excited. This was normal for them but totally new and incredible for me.

Our biggest adventure yet was when Bob took us on the family sailboat. This boat was so big, it had to be a dream. Bob gave me a life jacket and let me help raise the sail. Then, once we were out in the ocean away from the other boats, he showed me how to steer the boat all by myself. You couldn't tell me nothing. I could not wait to get back home and tell all my friends and family about my new life. Here I am, five years old, doing things that people in the projects 30+ years older have never done. Sailing was my bonding time with Bob. He worked a lot, which reminded me of my Dad. The difference was that Bob always made it home in time for dinner. He must have enjoyed Gail's cooking just as much as I did.

After several days, it was time for Gail and Jo to take me back to the train station to meet up with the Fresh Air Fund counselors. This was very sad for me, although I was homesick. I knew that the environment back in the projects would not compete with my new life here in Sea Cliff.

Gail saw the sadness in my eyes, and she bent down to hug me. "Nikki, you can come back anytime. I'll see you next year."

This was the beginning of many summers spent in Sea Cliff, New York. And the Lafferty's and my family even became family. That next year, I ended up staying past two weeks and stayed for a month. That summer, we had a big Fourth of July barbeque in the yard with fireworks. Everyone was there to welcome me back, so I felt very special. In the middle of the party, I saw the Fresh Air Fund counselors and some of the other Fresh Air Fund kids had arrived. Apparently, they came to get me because the other kids were homesick and wanted to go do something alone as a group. "I'm staying here with my family," my six-year-old self said to the counselor assertively.

I don't know if the other kids bonded with the families they were placed with, but I loved mine and I was not going anywhere! After that, we no longer used the Fresh Air Fund. The Lafferty's would just come down to the city and pick me up in downtown Manhattan at the Port Authority Terminal.

One particular year, they were coming to get me, and my Mom and I were prepared to go meet them at Port Authority. This was the time before cell phones when you couldn't give real-time updates of where you were. My house phone rang, and it was Gail.

"Hey Nikki. We're here," she said, and I am thinking 'oh my goodness!' "You're already at Port Authority?" I asked.

"No, we're outside of your building" she replied. Outside of the building?!!!

I threw my head outside of the window, and although I lived on the fifteenth floor, I could see they were right on the corner near the payphone - my White family, in the Harlem projects! I almost passed out.

"Ma!" I screamed. "They're outside! Downstairs!"
"Go get them! Go get them!" my Mom yelled.

I lived in the projects and it was not safe for White people in the late 80's to be standing on that corner. I ran down fifteen flights of stairs. There was no time to wait for the elevator.

"Nobody better not hurt my White family," I kept saying over and over as I ran down all those flights of stairs.

I was ready to fight any crackhead, knucklehead, thug, or anybody who thought of trying to hurt my White family - a family who had done nothing but love me. I was about nine years old at the time, but I felt I could beat anybody that day who even tried it. Don't get offended because I call them my White family. I loved them dearly, as if we had the same blood running through our veins. I say "White family" just because they were White. Color did not matter to me beyond a physical description. Jo was just my other sister, and Gail and Bob were just my other Mom and Dad.

Gail and Bob's hearts were so big, they even adopted a boy named Max a few years after I had started coming there. Having this little baby boy around, and helping take care of him, was such a joy because I was so used to being the youngest. I have always been the youngest, from being the youngest amongst my siblings, to being the youngest in my group to join the military and being the youngest on my unit to become an L&D nurse. Even to this day, when I want my way, I say, 'Uh, uh! I'm the baby. I ain't doin' that".

But Max was like a live baby doll. He was so handsome, and he cried a lot in the beginning. We still loved him anyway. Adopting Max just further showed me how great my host family was, and I am so forever grateful for them—for opening their hearts to me. I visited them every year from age five to age twelve, until my mother started sending me to visit my maternal grandmother in North Carolina during the summers, because I had two cousins down there around my age. I somehow lost contact with Gail, Bob, and Jo until three years ago when I decided to go searching for Gail on Facebook. I could not find Jo because I didn't know she had married and changed her last name.

"Nikki! Is that you?!" Gail wrote me after I messaged her on Facebook.

"Yes, it's me," I said, relieved to be reconnected again. I began to tell her all the good times I remembered. A few hours later, Gail posted a photo of Jo, herself, Bob, and I, and tagged me.

"Oh my God Nikki!!!! Is that you?!" one old friend from Sea Cliff exclaimed in the comments box.

"Nikki!!! We were wondering . . . 'What ever happened to that little girl Nikki'," another blast-from-the-past wrote.

It was a little Sea Cliff family reunion on Facebook. So many people liked the picture Gail posted and commented. I have been reconnected with Jo ever since and we talk on the phone often, but still have not had the chance to get together and meet because we both are busy with our kids! Time flies!

Those summers in Sea Cliff, compared to summer days in the New York projects, were at opposite ends of the spectrum. For example, I remember a nice summer day in the projects, and everyone was outside. I was on my roller skates, and my best friend, Denise was riding her bike. Her mom was nearby, watching us skate and ride back and forth. At one point, we took a break, and I was sitting on a bench, while Denise was sitting on her bike in front of me. Suddenly, we saw men coming through the park with towels wrapped around some long objects. I was ten, but I quickly figured out that the objects were shotguns and Uzi guns.

Over 100 kids and adults were around talking, laughing, playing cards, relaxing on the benches, rolling dice, and kids were playing as kids do. As the men approached, people started realizing what was wrapped inside of the towels and started scattering.

"Run!!!" Denise's mom, DeDe, told us. They both had the same name, so Denise's mom was "DeDe"for short.

Denise started riding her bike so fast, while I started skating away as fast as I could. The men were trying to get past us to the building behind us, but, before we could even get ten feet away, the shooting began.

"Ahhhhh! Boom! Boom! Boom! Pop! Pop!" All you heard was people screaming, rapid gunfire from the Uzis, and booming noises from the shotguns.

"Get down!" DeDe yelled. Denise screamed "Ma! Stop being nosy!" DeDe quickly shouted back "Shut up!! I'm trying to figure out which way the bullets are coming from!"

After seeing we were not in the line of fire, we began to run again. DeDe was running, I was skating fast, and Denise was pedaling the fastest I had ever seen her pedal in life. We could have been in the Olympics! However, it was just the speed and skill you get when your life is in danger. We made it to my best friend's building safely, but that was just one of the many gunfire wars in my projects.

CHAPTER 2
S.E.T. (SURVIVE, ESCAPE, TELL)

For a time, it was not easy to talk about what I am about to talk about next. However, I will, because if it might help someone else, then it is worth telling. I was in the eighth grade and I was thirteen years old. I had a homework assignment that I was taking to finish at Carmen's place, another best friend's house. Carmen did not live in the projects. She lived in a nice building a few blocks away. She had a doorman and lived on Fifth Avenue. That's the thing about Manhattan; you have your poor parts, middle class, and rich all in one borough. The other boroughs are all the same, but Manhattan is known as "Money Making Manhattan."

I was on my way home, and as I approached my building, I checked my surroundings. I saw a man that looked out of place. I did not recall ever seeing him in my neighborhood, but he was sitting on a bench, seemingly minding his own business. Therefore, I did not get too alarmed, and just kept walking towards my building. It was still daylight outside and there were a lot of people out.

The way the doors to my building are, you have to walk through one door and then the second door is locked. You must have a key to get in or you must ring the buzzer for someone to open the door. I had my key, but the door that was supposed to be locked, was not locked. I opened the second door, heard it slam shut, and then heard it open again. I quickly turned around and saw it was that out-of-place man coming through the door. The hallway was crowded with a whole bunch of people waiting for the elevator. We had two elevators. Both finally came down at the same time and the

15

people piled into them. Both elevators were full. I managed to get on one elevator, and the man got on the same one I did. As the elevator went up, people were getting off on each of their floors and the last person got off on the twelfth floor. Now, it was just me and the man remaining, and I had three more floors to go.

He moved to the back of the elevator and turned his back to me. When he turned back around, he had a knife. He put the knife to my chest and told me not to scream. Could this really be happening to me? The elevator opened on the fifteenth floor and he made me get off the elevator. He took me into the stairwell and up to the rooftop landing. Any other day, there would at least be crackheads in the stairwell, but not this time. He fondled my breasts as he knelt in front of me, now at eye level with my 4'11" frame. He kissed and licked my face and my breasts. Then, he grabbed my butt and pressed against me. He put the knife down on the ledge.

This was my opportunity to hit him in the nuts and run, but he was so tall and strong. I did not want him to grab the knife and hurt me because, at this point, I am thinking I am still alive and although disgusted by him and his touching . . . again . . . I am still alive. I even thought to grab the knife off the ledge myself, stab him, and run, but he was so powerful-looking that I did not want to risk getting hurt. Then, suddenly, we heard something below us. We both shot glances at the floor.

"Don't say anything," he looked at me and said. But then he got nervous.

"We should go, and see each other another time," I whispered, trying to trick him. My street smarts and survival skills kicked into gear. His sick-self thought I actually liked him, but I was just trying to live.
"Don't tell anyone," he said.

"Okay."

"Give me your phone number."

"Will I see you again?" I asked, faking interest, just going along with the flow of the conversation to make it out of there.

"Yeah."

I was so nervous that I wrote my real house phone number on my homework that I had just finished at Carmen's and gave it to him. He walked ahead of me, then ran down the stairs. I went immediately to my apartment. I had my house key but was shaking too badly to open the door. So finally, I knocked, and my sister, Rochelle, answered.

Growing up, everywhere my sister went, my Mom made her take me with her, but if you ever ask her, she did not mind because I was a good little sister. My sister did homework with me, cooked for me, and taught me cheerleading routines. I was so glad she was home. I knew everything would be all right if I could just get to her. She opened the door and I saw she was on the phone with her boyfriend. I pretended everything was okay. I came in and locked both locks behind me. We also have a police bar for the door. I made sure I put it in place. A police bar is a steel pole that you anchor on the floor and put it up against the door from the inside. It prevents anyone from kicking your door down or breaking in.

Once the bar was in place, I shot my eyes back up to my sister, who had begun walking down the hallway back to her bedroom and screamed her name uncontrollably.

"Roieeeeee!!!!" I started crying and yelled my sister's nickname. And, then I vomited, sick to my stomach from what had just happened.

"I have to hang up! Something happened to my sister!
I have to call 911!" she screamed into the phone.

I tried to calm down and tell her what happened, but I could not. I just kept
crying and vomiting. The police were on their way. I calmed down a little
enough to tell my sister that someone grabbed me in the hallway and took
me up to the roof landing. As there were no cellphones at this time, my
sister could not get in contact with our Mom. And, my Mom and Dad were
not together at this point. My Mom was engaged to my soon-to-be
stepfather.

The police arrived and took my statement. While taking my statement, my
sister's boyfriend came to our apartment, and walked in because the front
door was open. The detectives got all nervous and started grabbing on him.

"No, no, no!" I yelled. "That's my sister's boyfriend! That's not him! That's
not the man who hurt me!"

The ambulance and EMTs came and took me to the hospital. Even though
there was no penetration, they still performed a rape kit on me, which just
made me feel so dirty. My sister stayed with me the whole time, and while
we were waiting for the results, my Mom came through the door. When she
saw me, she just broke down and started crying and holding onto me.

"Was there penetration?" she asked the hospital staff.
"No," I quickly responded, and we just sat there crying together.

There was an investigation, and I ended up having to draw a sketch of the
man. They were able to find him, arrest him, and the case went to court.

Not able to afford a lawyer, we were assigned a court-appointed lawyer, and she lost the case. I was 100% sure that was the man who hurt me. I had spent so much time with him, from the elevator, to the stairwell, to the rooftop, and during the conversation back and forth.

 But my lawyer was not able to convince the jury that I was 100% sure. She made so many mistakes.

"Did he have a beard like this man?" asked the police sketch artist who sat down with me, going through description after description.

"Yes," I replied. To this day, I don't like men beards to put their mouths on my breasts. It reminds me of this terrible man scratching my chest with his horrible stubble for what seemed like eternity.

"Was his face long like this or short like this??", the sketch artist continued.

"It was long like that one."

"Did he have big eyes like these or small ones like these?" the sketch artist questioned, as she went on and on, until we had narrowed down every possible feature of a face that could be described.

Most of the jury believed everything I said, and that I had identified the right man, but one juror was not sure, because I was so strong on the witness stand. That juror felt I should have been crying and that I should have been nervous and afraid.

Well, that juror did not know this thirteen-year-old. Number one, my Mom was breaking down in the courtroom, so I knew I had to be strong for her. And, number two, I had to make sure I told them what he did to me clearly and concisely to make sure this animal would be locked away and never be able to hurt anyone else again. So, no... I did not cry, nor did I stutter.

I looked him in his eyes while I told them what he did to me. Some victims never get to confront their attacker. I refused to live my life in fear, so I made sure he knew that I was not afraid of him. I especially was not afraid at that moment because all my family members and my sister's boyfriend were there in the courtroom that day. I was even annoyed on the stand while testifying because I felt my attorney was not asking me the right questions. She was frazzled and overwhelmed, shuffling around with her papers. I was not represented well at all.

When I was cross-examined by his public defender, I destroyed him. I tore his questions to pieces. Yes, I was only thirteen years old, but I must have been a lawyer in my other life. The way I answered those questions, he had no case. But, again, it was that one juror that my lawyer just could not convince. They found him not guilty.

After the case, I found out that I was not his only victim. He had been doing things to his girlfriend's kids. He would drill holes in the walls to watch her kids in their bedroom. He was just a sick individual - a pedophile. All I know is that after that day in court, I never saw him again.
If someone has ever hurt you, I urge you to always tell someone. Do not hold it in, no matter how you feel. Do not try to hide it. Do not feel ashamed by it. The only way to heal is to face it. I thank God that *He* gave me the wisdom to have those survival skills. I thank God that I could tell my sister. I would not be silent. I would not live in fear. That is what I pray for anyone who is reading this and has been through something similar, or who has been through something with anyone who has hurt that person in any kind of way.

Do not let them control your life. Do not let that situation control your life. Tell someone. Get the help you need. Get through it and help make sure it does not happen to someone else. It may take time, but make sure you are moving forward.

After my incident, my soon-to-be stepfather walked me to and from school every day. I thank him for that because he had back problems, and he used to really be in pain some mornings, but he pushed through the pain to make sure that I was safe. I will always appreciate him for that.

There are some steppingstones that you have to get over, but never stop going forward. We can change these kinds of attacks on children, one person at a time. I started making a difference and now it is your turn. Take back your life today! If that eighth grader could take her life back, then so can you!

In the ninth grade, in my freshman year of high school, I went to Saint Jean Baptiste in downtown Manhattan at an all-girls Catholic school. I was very athletic, so I was on the softball team, basketball team, and the volleyball team. I even helped the cheerleaders learn cheers for tryouts. I could not be on the cheerleading team because of the conflict with all the sports I was playing. But high school was a great time. I was never one of those kids that wanted to grow up fast. I enjoyed being in high school.

Ninth grade was a fun year. I mean, we had the best era of music in the 90's. In downtown Manhattan, off 75th Street, we had a store called "HMV." This was a music store where celebrities would come and you would get to meet them, get their autographs, and sign their CDs. When I met Whitney Houston, there were so many people in line that it was wrapped around the whole block. The store itself had two floors and it was still packed in there. Two news helicopters kept hovering to video the massive amount of people there to meet Whitney.

I met many celebrities just living in New York. I met TLC, the girl group. It happened in the last weeks of my eighth-grade year. We had just gotten our class rings. One tradition was that each person would turn your ring on your finger the number of times that equaled the year you graduated. So, if you graduated in 1998, you would go around and have 98 different people each turn the ring around your finger once and one time for good luck. TLC was the last of the people to turn my ring. I got to meet each of them T-Boz, Left Eye, and Chilli.

Then, I went to my first, real high school party, with my friends Denise and Carmen. I have known Denise since three and Carmen since five. The music was so good, and the DJ was hot. He had everybody on the dance floor, from the time we got there, until the time we left. At one point none of the guys would dance with me and I was wondering what was going on.

"A guy likes you, so he told everybody not to dance with you," one of my guy friends finally told me. And, I'm looking like 'y'all listened to him?'

I knew who the guy was. He was my old classmate's older brother. At the end of the party, a fight broke out in the vestibule of the building, so we were kind of pushed back into the gym of the school until security broke it up. They kicked the fighting people out. After it was clear, we started walking towards the exit. That is when I saw the guy who liked me, standing outside.

"Come here," he told me. But, when I turned around, I saw that my friends were not right behind me, so I told him to hold on, and I went back to get my friends. I was a little nervous because this guy was two years older than me and way more experienced, if you catch my drift. I retrieved my friends, then on my way out of the building I tried to walk right past him.

"Nicole!!" he called out so loud and authoritatively. I immediately went over to him. He asked for my beeper number and he gave me his - boy am I telling my age. So, after we exchanged numbers, my best friends and I started walking away from the party. Right, when we got across the street, the guys that got kicked out for fighting, pulled up in a car, got out, and popped the trunk. Once again, my street smarts kicked in. I know what that means when somebody in the hood speeds up and jumps out to pop the trunk.

I told my friends to walk fast and that's one thing about people in my culture - when you tell them to do something like run or walk fast, they do not ask questions. They just do it. As we scurried past them, the guys took guns out of the trunk and passed them out to each other. Simultaneously, a big ole' New York City rat jumped out of the garbage.

"Ahhhhhh!" my friends and I screamed. We screamed so loudly that everybody's attention drew to us. "These big ass rats almost ran over our feet!" I exclaimed. I quickly cleaned it up so the guys would not think we were screaming about their guns.

Yes, I cussed, but it was because I had to blend into the environment. I am not even a person who cusses. A few words will slip out here and there, but I really do not have a potty mouth. That is what my elementary teacher used to warn us about.

"People who cuss a lot are ignorant and they don't have a broad vocabulary", she told us. From that day forward, I always made sure I articulated everything I said, and got my point across firmly, without using cuss words. But, this time, cuss words were called for.

"Yo! There they go!" some kids out front yelled after seeing the guys with their guns. I told my girls to run, and we ran down Lexington Avenue towards Denise's house.

Then, it started. We heard the rapid gunfire erupt behind us from the oozies and the 'pow,' 'pow,' 'pow' from the regular handguns as we ran away from the scene. Then, after two blocks of running, Carmen had an asthma attack right when we had reached the '6' train on Lexington Avenue.

"Carmen! Carmen! Get up please! Get up! You have to run!" I shouted to her. She just kept puffing.

"I can't breathe," she wheezed. But I just did not want to catch a bullet that did not have my name on it.

"Are y'all OK?" We suddenly heard a man's voice right behind us just then. He had followed us.

"Ahhhh!" we screamed immediately in shock. But it was a guy Carmen knew. A guy that liked Carmen, in fact, and who Carmen liked back. He saw us running away as he started to run, so he ran after us to protect us. I do not know how he was able to do that, however. Because from the direction he came, he would have had to run straight through the bullets!

He was older than us - a senior in high school. But he and Carmen never became a thing because back at that age, that was considered a huge age difference if you were a freshman or even a sophomore while the guy was a senior in high school.

"No, we're not ok. She's having an asthma attack", I said.
"Well, y'all got to leave. It's not safe for y'all to be here."

He flagged down a cab and put us in a ride home. It was the one time I was thankful a man had followed us. There it was again, another shoot-out, and just eight blocks from home.

My mother knew things were getting worse in the city, so for the summers, she started sending me to Connecticut to stay with my grandmother's sister. I loved it up in Connecticut. I had a whole bunch of cousins that were my age. When we all got together for family functions up there, it was never less than 50 people. My grandmother's sister had five kids and a bunch of grandkids staying there. There was never a dull moment in Connecticut. My maternal grandmother has ten kids - six boys, four girls, and my Mom is the youngest of all of them. My Mom's side alone is huge.

My Mom would also send me to the Bronx to stay at my cousin Sharon's house because my cousin Tunisia who lived there was the same age as me. At times, my Mom would send me to New Jersey to stay with my Uncle Nick as well. I would babysit his boys so he and his wife, my aunt Joyce, could go out. Some summers, I would go to Maryland and stay with my Aunt Fran and Aunt Niecy, because they also had cousins my age with them. They used to live in the Bronx and, as a child, I would go there often.

Once they moved to Maryland, my Mom would send me out there during the summer too.

In life, you just work with what you got and make the best of it. That's one of the lessons I learned from my mother. My Mom tried to keep me out of the projects as best she could. Growing up, my Mom had me at the Boys' and Girls' Club, which was right around the corner from our house, where I took ballet classes. She tried to expose me to different things despite where we lived.

Most little kids in my neighborhood didn't get the chance to experience the culture on Broadway. Going to Broadway, to watch all the beautiful shades of black skin dancing across the stage in Alvin Ailey plays, showed me that Black people were doing more than selling drugs or shaking their butts to music. My Aunt Jannie lived with us when I was in the second grade. She was an actress and I went to her plays. At one particular play, I was sitting right in the front row when, in one scene, one of the male actors had to slap my Aunt for her to fall down and start crying.

"Don't hit my Auntie!" I yelled out, and the whole place roared.
I may have been only seven, but I knew no man should be putting his hands on a woman. After the play was over, they took me backstage to show me that it was fake, and that the slap sound was made with sound effects. But I just didn't get it.

My Mom also put me in Girl Scouts. I applaud those counselors. They were white, middle-aged women who would come into Spanish Harlem, and expose us girls to a whole other way of living. They taught us to cook healthier with what we could afford, took us hiking, and registered us for Girl Scouts' camp. I was also in PAL, which is the Police Athletic League–

another organization that keeps at-risk youth involved in multiple activities to keep them off the streets.

My Dad lived off Edgecombe Avenue. My sister and I loved being at my Dad's house. He also was tired of the violence that was going on where I lived, so he used to send me down to North Carolina for some of the summer to stay with two of his sisters and his mother. They all had their own houses.

But I loved being around my grandmother the most. My grandmother had a garden outside. We were out there picking green beans and peas, which was a big deal for this city girl. After picking them, we went inside the house and started snapping them open. I must have been about eight. My grandmother took them over to the sink to rinse them off.

"What are you doing Grandma?" I asked.
"We are about to cook them so we can eat them."
"Those just came from outside in the dirt, we not eating those. Green beans and peas come from a can", I said matter-of-factly. When I tell you, they just started laughing at me . . . this city girl had so much to learn.

When my Mom got married to my stepfather, we relocated to Jacksonville, Florida. I wanted to stay in New York with my sister, but my grandmother was not having that. After summer was over, I moved to Jacksonville with my mother and her husband.

Of course, when I got there, I hated it because it was so country. I wasn't just visiting… I had to live there. Talking about moving somewhere new and not knowing anyone as a teenager. What a disruption! I was upset that my grandmother made me come live with my Mom. I was fine in New

York. I was used to the projects at that time. But it did not take me long to
make friends in Florida. It is a gift that I have always been very social.
New Yorkers tend to gravitate to each other when in other states. One
friend, whom I was close with from New York, was one of the first girls I
met at school when we moved, and she was good people. Unfortunately,
she was accidentally killed because a family member about her age was
playing with a gun when it went off and shot her in the face. The
ambulance came quickly, but could not get inside the apartment in time,
because they received the call as "Shots Fired". This meant they had to wait
for the police to come before they could enter. That complex was just that
dangerous. That had become the protocol. That complex had barbed wire
and what looked like jail gates.

It was very tragic because we were so young and people our age aren't
supposed to die. She always went to school. She made good grades. And,
she helped her Mom out with her little sister. She was very responsible and
a beautiful soul. We were supposed to walk across the stage together for
graduation. The hardest part was when we had a memorial for her in the
school. I just lost it then because I finally came to the realization that my
friend was gone. Tomorrow isn't promised and death has no age restriction.
If I learned anything at that age, I learned not to take life for granted. I
mean, she was not in the wrong place at the wrong time. She was at her
home. She was not out doing the wrong things. She was just simply sitting
in her room on her telephone when it happened.

From that point onward, I was motivated to make sure I always did the best
I could in life. And, I will always keep pushing forward because not
everyone is given the chance to do things later as later may never come. Her
life was taken. The realization that she would not walk down the graduation

aisle with me, that she would never get married, that she would never have kids—I was so devastated. Her whole life stopped at 17 years old. Life can be taken away at any moment, so my question is always, 'Are we walking in purpose or are we just existing?'

Three weeks before high school graduation, I overheard an Army Recruiter talking to one of my friends about becoming an LPN (Licensed Practical Nurse) for the Army. Here I was, so adamant about going to Virginia State University (VSU) to become a child psychologist. I picked that field because of my tragic pedophile attack in New York. I wanted to be a help to children, in particular, to get through and live their lives to the fullest - not in shame, blame, or fear.

I had applied to VSU, gotten accepted, and everything. But, upon listening to the benefits of joining the Army, I found out that the military would pay me on the first and fifteenth of every month while studying to become a nurse and pay for my license as well. My little car had to pump the breaks and I put myself in reverse! 'Getting paid to go to school?' I thought. So, I signed up. I received a very high score on the Army's ASVAB placement test and could have gotten any kind of job I wanted, but I decided to pursue nursing.

At the end of training, Capt. Peterson, told me to apply to Hampton University and obtain my Bachelor's degree. So, that's just what I did. This little project girl, the same little project girl that people and society told would never amount to anything, became more than something.

"You're just gonna grow up and stay in the system your whole life just like the rest of these project people," they would say. "You're going to raise generation, after generation, after generation right there in those projects."

I guess sometimes you have to show them better than you can tell them. But, by no means am I taking credit for the progression of my life. That was all God and I am thankful! How powerful it can be, just being taken out of one's environment and put into another . . . affording you the opportunity to see past your current situation! Think of a time when someone took you out of your environment and put you into another one—one that had a positive impact on your life. It could have been for a short or long time, but that was enough for me to know that if I was not exposed to all the things I was exposed to, and when I was exposed to them, that I would not have been open enough to accept all the good things waiting to happen in my life.

CHAPTER 3
GIFT OF GAB

I finally arrived at Hampton University in Virginia. College was going great. I lived in the dorms for one semester and then I moved into an apartment fifteen minutes from campus. This place was so much different than being in the Army. For starters, I did not have to do a Physical Fitness training three days a week. I did not have any extra duties. I could just go to class and study. So, of course, I made the Dean's List every semester. I was used to having such a heavy load from learning to be a soldier and how to become a nurse. Now, all I had to do was focus on school.

Once again, the New Yorkers flocked to each other. I met a guy from Queens, New York who I called 'Queens'. True to Gemini form, he had the gift of gab and was known for using this gift to talk girls out of their panties soon after meeting him. But that wasn't happening here. He asked for my number. I told him no and that I was in a long-distance relationship at the time.

"Talk to my roommate instead," I told him. They hung out from time to time. I was in my own little world. But then she started talking to someone else and she and Queens stopped talking.

My boyfriend at the time had come down to visit me at college and surprised me during homecoming. But, my friend Inala from high school was already visiting me. He knocked and my roommate answered the door. Inala and I were in my room with the door closed and the TV blasting, so we did not hear the door. Next thing I know, my room door flies open, and it is him. I immediately jumped up off my bed and ran into his arms. Inala grabs her stuff fast and moves to the living room. She knew I had not seen him in months.

Inala later went with my friends to a party, which I did not go to because I wanted to stay and spend time with my boyfriend. But Inala did not feel comfortable spending the night at my friends' house because she had just met them. So, she called me to come and get her, although the original plan was for her to spend the night there. As such, it was 3 o'clock in the morning when she called for me to come get her. But my friend did not live that far away - maybe fifteen minutes.

I did not wanna wake my boyfriend up because he had a long drive back in the morning. So, I just went and got her, and brought her back to my house. When the morning came and my boyfriend found out I had left in the middle of the night, he insisted that I must be cheating and messing around. Needless to say, if you do not have trust in a relationship then there is no relationship.

"I can't do this. I don't trust you being up here in college with all of these college guys", he said. We broke up and he just stopped calling.

But I am the type of person that does not cheat, and I have never cheated, because I feel like we are all adults. If I do not want to be with you, I can just come and say I do not want to be with you. I have never been the type of person that wants to date two men at the same time. His words made me feel dirty. Sharing my body with two different men - one night with one and the next night with the other - is not me. Even though they would not be with me at the same time, I would still feel like they were running a train on me. I do not play games with men's hearts, especially because I do not want men playing with mine. Now, that I am older, I can see that when a person accuses you of cheating, sometimes it is actually that person doing the cheating. I think, in that case, he was. I know who I am. I do not have to cheat. If I do not want to be with you anymore, too bad.

"Hey, how you doing?" came Queens's voice on the other end of the line in a surprise call from him months later. It was the guy that I had rejected and pushed off to my roommate.

I was home watching TV and did not catch most of what he was saying in the beginning. So, I started having a completely different conversation.

"Are you with anyone?" is what I thought Queens asked me.
"No, I am single," I said and proceeded to go on with this whole extra story of my ex, blah, blah, blah.
"Okay," he said.
"Wait a minute. What did you ask me?" I tried to correct myself.
"I said are y'all doing anything fun over there?" Immediately, we started laughing so hard. We laughed for a good two minutes. At the time, my roommate was out with her boyfriend.

"Sorry to talk your ear off," I apologized. "I misunderstood the question. I heard something else.

"My roommate is out and I'll have her call you back." We hung up and then about ten minutes later the phone rings back and it is him.

"One of my friends here from New York is throwing a party. Since you're from New York and all, do you want to go?", he asked. I had not been anywhere in months, so I thought to myself, "I'm young. Let me go out and hang around some new people." And, that's just what I did.

We actually had a really good time at the party. The DJ was really good, and he was from New York also. I was getting numbers and Queens was getting numbers. We joked, laughed, and danced together. We just had a really good time. After that, he invited me to a couple more events and, again, it was the same - we always had a good time.

Then, one day, he approached me about being in a relationship and I told him I had to talk to my roommate because, even though they never had anything together, I did not want to start liking him in that way if she had any feelings left for him. She had to be cool with it.

He totally understood and actually called my roommate to talk to her and tell her that he had feelings for me and would like to pursue me, but he did not want it to be weird and he did not want her to think that we had anything before they were talking. She told him she did not mind and that it sounded like we had more in common and had more fun together anyway. Then, I spoke with her next.

"I have never done anything like this before. I know we are grown, but I just wanted to make sure it was okay."

"Girl, it's fine," she said and so that is how my first relationship in Virginia began.

Things were great. We really had good times together. We would go out and have fun. We spent a lot of time together. He worked hard. I worked hard in school and got good grades. That first year was so blissful. I used to go to every basketball game he had on the Navy base and he was a really good basketball player. Basketball is my favorite sport. That is the case, especially coming from New York, because all the kids in my neighborhood grew up playing basketball as there were so many basketball courts in every park in the projects.

The end of my lease soon arrived and so I moved into Queen's place. That is when I became pregnant with my first-born. Shortly after my first trimester, a woman called the house and asked for him. I picked up the call because at that time we still just had house phones. I told him he had a phone call, but I just had this gut feeling that something was not right. Maybe it was the tone of surprise of the woman when I picked up. I listened to my gut and pretended to hang up the phone but continued listening to the conversation.

"So, you live with a girl now?"
"No, that's just my friend," Queens said.
"Oh really, I'm just your friend?" I jumped into the conversation. The girl gasped and he hung up the phone and immediately came into the room to where I was.

"I am leaving you. I can't believe you would do this to me and when I'm having your baby. I will not be cheated on."

"Please stay," he cried as he got on his knees and begged. "I love you and I want to be a part of my child's life. This girl doesn't mean anything to me. I don't even know why I gave her my number. I'm so stupid for jeopardizing what we have. If you give me another chance, I will never do something like this again."

This begging and pleading went on for hours so I decided to give him one more chance since this would be his first-born son and my first-born child. So, yes, I stayed because I did not want to raise a baby by myself, especially my first baby and especially with no other family living in the immediate area and none even in the same state.

We moved from his apartment into a rented townhome in both of our names. I cooked five days a week and studied six days a week, feeding my nursing friends about three to four times a week because we always had study groups at my house.

I started working at the VA Veterans' Hospital when I was about three months pregnant. There were men there who had served in our military, gone to war, and lost their legs or other limbs. They were unable to walk or take care of themselves. It was an honor to take care of them and to hear their stories.

Going to nursing school full-time and feeling things were so hard trying to balance work and school, were nothing compared to what the veterans had been through. I would look at them and see how much they sacrificed so that I could have the freedoms that I had and now have.

Queens was active duty during this time so we would share my vehicle for him to get back and forth to work. And, sometimes he would drop me off at work on the weekends when he did not have to work. Here, is where the problem started.

Queens started his bad habits again. He would pick me up from work late, almost every weekend. One weekend, when I was eight months pregnant, I was sitting outside with one of the veterans waiting for what seemed like forever and having just worked a 12-hour shift. I was so disappointed. You know when your gut is telling you one thing, but your heart keeps telling you to ignore it? There were definitely signs - signs that I wish my heart had not told me to ignore.

Riding with my friend Amber one day to her apartment, I saw my SUV and a female sitting in the backseat of it. I am eight and a half months pregnant at this point, but don't you know I still ran up to the door and swung it open, and hard. Of course, Queens is there with her and looked startled as usual as if he could never get caught. She was startled, too.

"Who you got in my SUV?!"

"Oh, this is my friend. She just needed a ride and that's why she's sitting in the backseat. I don't want you to think nothing."

"Young lady, you got to walk, because me and him got issues. This is not his vehicle and I do not know you," I felt the need to explain to her. Queens did not attend Hampton University, but as much as he was on that campus you would have thought he was a student. He was just lurking around trying to pick up girls. Still, this incident was not enough to end our relationship.

Three days before my due date, I woke up with contractions, although I did not know they were contractions. All I knew is that I felt like I had to use the bathroom every five minutes, and I don't mean emptying my bladder. After getting up to go to the bathroom the third time with no results, I thought to myself, 'Hmm, I might be having contractions.'

It was Easter Sunday and my mother had just come down two days prior to spend Easter with me. Just the day before, I had been very active. We went to the commissary to go shopping for groceries, and we also picked up the baby shower gifts that my sister had sent. We had been out and about all day just the day before, but I later found out that the burst of energy I felt was called 'nesting.' It is when a woman gets a burst of energy just before she goes into labor - like adrenaline.

"Mom, I think I'm having contractions," I said as I woke my mother up. I thought she was just going to tell me to lay back down. That's what she told my sister, Rochelle, when she was having her son.

"Ok, let's go in!" she said instead. But then I paused. Is this really happening? I called my doctor and they told me to come into labor and delivery.

When I checked in, I was only one centimeter, so they had me walk the hallways for two hours. Then, when they rechecked me, I was three centimeters, so they admitted me. My Mom called my sister Rochelle, who was living in Florida at the time, and told her that they admitted me to the hospital. My sister called out of work and she and my ten-year-old nephew drove all the way to Virginia. That's right. I'm the baby of the family, the youngest of four kids and everybody in my family spoils me.

After a few hours of being admitted, I got some pain medicine through an IV. This medicine was so strong that it would bring me in and out of consciousness. Sometimes I would wake up and see our friends there and then other times I would wake up and only see my son's godmother, Amber, with Queens.

"Every time you wake up, you keep rambling on about food," they laughed. I was not allowed to eat, and you know I love to eat. That is why I was not excited to be in labor on Easter Sunday, with my Mom cooking Cornish hens, baked macaroni and cheese, sweet potatoes, collard greens, pot roast, and string beans. I was not going to be able to eat any of it. My mom was going back and forth to the hospital because she was still cooking and trying to be there for my delivery at the same time.

"Just go ahead and cook the food," I said. "Don't worry about me. Just cook the food." I got all the way up to eight centimeters, and then I asked for my epidural.

"You really want it?" the nurse asked me. She looked at me surprised, because I was doing so well.

"I can have one, right?" I asked.

"Yeah, I'll get it."

But the real truth is that I could have made it without it because I basically slept through the whole epidural. I remember sitting up to say something about not letting me move and then that was it. I do not remember anything else that happened until the nurse woke me up to push. Amber stood by my side and Queens on the other side. For the first 30 minutes, I was not pushing correctly because the epidural was so strong. I was not pushing in the right spot and then my doctor motioned for the nurse to turn off my epidural.

"No, Nancy," I told the nurse holding onto her arm as she reached for the epidural. "The doctor doesn't mean it," I said deliriously. She just laughed and turned off the epidural. They then allowed me to rest for fifteen minutes and then we began to push again. Without the epidural, I started to feel the pressure from the contractions. My doctor was the coolest.

"Reach down and pull your son out," the doctor said once my son had come out up to his shoulders. So, I reached down, pulled him out, and put him on my belly. All of the emotions and pride I felt at having birthed a little human being was so beautiful and amazing. But then, I noticed my son was not crying, which meant he was not breathing.

"Why is he not crying?" I questioned. But when I asked this question, it was as if my son heard me. He suddenly gave a little whimper of a cry. Then, we all started crying. He had my eyes - these big ole beautiful eyes.

My sister drove from Jacksonville, Fl to Hampton, VA, and missed the delivery by 45 minutes. If my mom would have called her when I first went to the hospital, Rochelle would have made it. My Mom did, however, get to videotape the delivery, and my sister got to see it. Amber was on my right-hand side and Queens was on my left-hand side the whole time. It was a great and wonderful experience coming into motherhood.

My mother went back to my house and fixed me a big ole Easter dinner plate, and when it arrived, I was so hungry. But I literally could not eat more than two bites of everything. I was so upset that I got full so fast and could not eat more. My stomach just would not let me.

I was at the end of my junior year of nursing school when I had my son, so I did not go to class for one whole week.

"Do not go visit Nicole at the hospital or her house. She needs to rest," one of our professors told my nursing classmates.
"They ain't gonna tell me I can't come up here and see you," said my classmate Katina as she busted into the hospital room the next day.

Once I got home, the majority of my nursing friends came right over to pick up our study group where we had left off. There were eleven of them all at my house that whole week, asking me to explain the study guide and the notes to prepare for finals. I was still cooking for them, too. It was wild. But it reassured me that everyone loved me. Until Katina told me that the professors told them they could not come and visit me, I had been thinking, 'What did I do to deserve to be left in this hospital like this without any visitors?' Plus, I always had a way of breaking things down to a level that they could understand so nursing study group would not go to anyone else. Another one of my gifts.

I returned to school that following Monday for finals. I brought my son with me and his car seat and took my nurse final just like that. I breastfed him and then the teacher took him and burped him and put him to sleep, back in his car seat. I am so thankful for those professors because if they saw that you were really trying hard, they would not get in your way. They would help you, and I do not think it would have been this way in any other university. Hampton University is special. No other nursing program would have done that for me. This is why I always encourage any mother to stay in school no matter what their situation might be. Don't stop. Keep going. It is possible to get there while pregnant and at a nursing program that is one of the top five, hardest to get through. Somehow you will find a way and find the right people to help you through it.

It would be wonderful to be able to tell you that we all lived happily ever after, after my first-born, but that would not be the truth. Six months later Queens's habits started changing again. He was staying out all night, claiming he had too much to drink and that he needed to stay at his friend's house to sober up. But he also had my car with him, so that left me and his son unable to get where we needed to go.

The number of times per week that Queens would go out and become unreachable started to increase week by week. One night, I would not let him borrow my car so someone else - one of his boys - picked him up. Then, that night, I waited up to see who was going to drop him off. Lo and behold, it was a female. I darted out the house towards the car and she sped off so fast.

"Come back here and take him with you!" I yelled at 3 o'clock in the morning. The whole neighborhood was quiet and should have been asleep, but I know they heard me that night. Queens hurried me up into the house.

"That was a friend and nothing more. She was the only one that could drop me off because my other friend had already left me there at the house party."

"I don't believe you! If that's your friend, why did she drive off so fast?!" I asked.
"She didn't think you would believe her, and she didn't want any problems", he explained.

"Well, if this is a friend then she should have no problem coming over to meet me to tell me that herself" I shot back.

"She's just a friend," he said. "I didn't even know her like that", he continued
"I don't believe you," I repeated.

Another two months later, he had my SUV again and my cell phone this time. He said he would be right back in an hour or two. But, after three hours, I began calling him because my son ran out of milk and I needed to go to the store and get more. Well, of course, Queens does not answer the phone. So, I start calling his friends, asking them if they know where he is.

"You're just trying to check on him," my son's godfather said when I called him. "Stop calling around to all his friends trying to check on him". I was really offended.

"No, I just need my vehicle because my son needs milk", I shot back. I ended up calling Ollecia, another nursing school friend, and she got out of her bed at 3 o'clock in the morning to buy my son some milk. I was so embarrassed, but she was a real friend and totally understood.

See, I had a whole village of nursing friends that were in my class that also became my family. They all would watch my son for me if I had class or clinicals, so he was kind of the nursing school baby. He was at every group study for the first year and a half of his life. I went through way more stuff with Queens, with late nights of him not coming home, or him not picking up the phone once he is out. I was tired, but, through all this heartache and stress, I still did my work, I still went to class, and I still held my study groups. I was determined not to let him mess up my plan of graduating and having a career that would afford a better life for me and my son.

I strive to be a good person to everyone I come in contact with. So, when someone is bringing negativity, I simply keep doing what I am supposed to be doing. I am not a woman who cheats or has ever cheated because, like I said, I am grown, and I can simply say "this is not gonna work anymore. We need to go our separate ways". In this case, I was not ready to give up on the relationship because I wanted my son to know that I gave 110%, trying to make things work between his father and me.

Most of Queen's friends would tell him that he was stupid and that I was a good woman. They would also tell him that as soon as I got my degree, I was going to leave him if he did not change. But, do you think he listened, or do you think he just tried to get away with more stuff?

Finally, graduation came. I actually finished a bachelor's program in three years because I went full-time even in the summers and, yes, I had a baby, and I worked. I knew it would all pay off. Nursing school is blood, sweat, and tears, quite literally. But, knowing that you will always have a job, being paid well, being able to choose different types of specialties, and traveling and living wherever you want to live while being independent, is priceless and well worth it.

Six months after my graduation, Queens decides to go to his co-worker's house to study for the next rank. He borrows my SUV and I get woken out of my sleep with a call around 2 o'clock in the morning from the Newport News Sheriff.

"Queens was in a car accident while coming from a party", the Sheriff told me.

"Is my car okay?" is the only question I could think to ask first, since he was not supposed to even be at no party.

"Do you mean, is *he* okay?" asked the Sheriff.

"No, is my car okay officer?" I repeated.

"Well, actually, no, it's not, and we have to tow it."

I am so disgusted at this point. Queens did not get home until about five in the morning. This is because a different Sheriff drove around with him in the car for a few hours just having an a man-to-man talk with him about how he could have died, how he could have lost his military career because he had been drinking, and how it is time to put childish things away and take care of business.

Queens told me he would get help with his drinking and that he would be a better man and a better father. So, yes, I gave him one more chance. My car was totaled, and I took responsibility because I should not have let him drive my car. I got another vehicle and I did not let him drive that one.

A week later, I wanted to go out with my friends because I never went out, and Queens was supposed to watch our son. I could not find him at first. So, I called to him and he was standing just outside the door.

"Queens?" I called.
"I'm going to the neighbor's house to talk. You could go. He's good."

"No, he's a toddler. Come inside and watch him in the house. What neighbor's house are you at? But, apparently, two doors down two college females moved in and he was in their doorway talking to them. So, I went off and started yelling.

"You talking to these chicks and you supposed to be watching your son! You are being disrespectful and irresponsible! It's not okay to leave a toddler in the house by himself!"
"Yeah? Who are you talking to like that?" he said embarrassed.

"I'm talking to you! You're not gonna leave my son in the house by himself!" Three of my girls was sitting in my SUV waiting for me, and two of his boys were standing outside talking, so Queens felt exposed.

"You not talking to me like that," he said and then he mushed me on the side of my head. 'Mush' is like a small push with one's hand.

"Did you just put your hands on me?! Go in the house!"

So, we went in the house and his friends went in the house and my female friends went in the house. I close the door and asked him again?

"Did you just hit me?" And, before he can get the whole word 'yeah' out his mouth, I drew my fist back and clocked him in his face. Now, I am 5'2 and he is 6'2, but my fist connected with the left side of his face and he stumbled back and fell on the floor.

"Ohhhhhhhhhhhh!!!" everyone shouted. Then, they all got in between the both of us and one of his friend's picked me straight up and took me outside.

"Girl, I will watch your son. Just go. You don't need to stay here right now." So, I left, and I went out with the girls for a few hours to get something to eat and to calm down because I did not want to let him bring me out of character like that any further. But, when you try to leave my child alone in the house and you mush me, you are going to see another side of me.

Two weeks after the incident, he stayed out all night again and came home as the sun came up. This was it. He walked in and I just smiled.

"Are you hungry?" I asked.
"No, I have to hurry up and get to work."
"Don't worry. I'll drop you off", I replied

"I have to take a quick shower", he said. While he was in the shower, I slipped his house key off his key ring and then I drove him to work.

"We will have a talk when I get home," he promised and then said, "I was at my female best friend Nae Nae's house."

I am not the jealous type. I met Nae Nae a lot of times when we went to New York to visit our families. Queens and Nae Nae had known each other for 15+ years. One time, when I had visited her, I told her she should try to find a job out here in Virginia and that she could stay with us until she found her own place. She did just that. She got the job in Virginia She moved down with us for a few months. Then, she bought a car and got her own place.

I love helping single mothers out no matter what, because sometimes you just need the right people around you to help you move out of a bad situation and onto the next level. Not everyone has a support system, so it is important to help whenever possible. She later thanked me for being a positive influence in her life when she was going through tough times. Nae Nae admired how I stood up for myself against men.

While Queens was at work, I took all his belongings and drove them over to Nae Nae's house, where he said he was at all night. I made sure he had everything that was his - all his clothes, sneakers, and his magazines. That is all he had. Everything else in the house was mine. He did not notice that I took the key off his key ring. I was fed up, and he had to go. He was probably at work telling Nae Nae 'yeah, everything is good' and 'I'll be over later so we can hang out again. Little did he know; I had kicked him out. Nae Nae broke the news to him.

"You know your girl bought everything over here and she said you could stay over here permanently?!" He was so devastated and embarrassed, but for how many months had I been devastated and embarrassed? I just didn't want any more of it. He got off work and found a ride home. He was banging on the door and ringing the bell 5,000 times, telling me to let him in and I kept telling him to go hang out in the streets.

"Don't try to come home now! You didn't respect me or the home we have so stop with all the dramatics."

He just banged harder and yelled harder and rang the doorbell more and more. So, I called his mother and told her what was happening.

Let me take a minute to honor this wonderful woman. My first conversation on the phone with her was after I found out that I was pregnant, and I had just moved in with him. She told me 'congratulations' and 'it was nice talking to you' over the phone, but it was not warm and fuzzy. Then, after the first time meeting her in person, both her and June, her husband, were very nice and welcoming. After I had her first grandson, because Queens was an only-child, me and her was closer than ever. If I had to describe it, we had a mother-daughter relationship. Queens was not the best at calling her and keeping in contact with her. She and I spoke almost every other day. He would call her every blue moon. So, when she heard the way he was banging on that door and ringing the doorbell and yelling at me to open the door, she was so angry with him.

"I wish you could open up the door and let me speak to him!" she said.
"I am not opening up the door for that angry black man on the other side."
After an hour or so, he finally left. He went to Nae Nae's house. After being over there another few days, I told him he is not coming back here.

"I am not moving", he stated.

"Okay. Then, my son and I will move. While I was moving your stuff out, I found naked pictures with different dates and different girls. One of them was that girl I caught you in my car with. The letters were talking about how you were together and about the sex you had", I informed him.

These dates were from the days after I had my son up until now.

This was definitely the last straw. I saw that he was never going to change. I had a choice to make and I had to choose me and my son. I did not want my son to grow up in a toxic environment. I did not want him to see his father cheating, not coming home, and not being responsible, while his mother was sad all the time. The double last straw was the fact that he allowed my son and I to move out, having to start all over again, rather than him moving. This man did not love me nor his first-born son. He clearly was not the one for me. He was beyond selfish, so I went looking, and found a townhouse.

When applying for the townhouse, something came up on my credit. "We cannot accept you because you have something on your credit," the lady at the rental office said.

"What is it? I always pay everything on time."
"It is a joint, jewelry credit card between you and your husband." The card had been paid off, but supposedly Queens lost the ring that I had gotten him. Without me knowing, he went to the jewelry store and bought the ring back.

"I had no idea about it. I will go and take my name off that credit card."

"You also have to promise not to let him move in with you," she said. I assured her that it was over between him and I and that he would never live with me there. She trusted me and approved me for the townhouse.

The next day, I called the movers and they came and packed up all my stuff, taking apart my bedroom set and my son's crib. They took everything that belonged to me, which were the couches, the TVs, the dressers, the whole kitchen set, and they put it all back together at my new townhouse.

My son and I started our new life together and that was the first time I became a single Mom. It was not easy being a nurse and working 12-hour shifts and working nights. But I am thankful I found a nighttime babysitter. My coworkers also helped me out from time to time because they worked dayshift. I would bring my son into work and then my coworker Marcus would take my son home with him and bring him back in the morning. I must say, God always provided me with a village.

Can you describe or name a person from your past or in your current life who, no matter how many chances you gave them, they never became the person that you deserved?

Can you name a person from your past or in your current life that did not love you the way you should have been loved and they always put themselves first?

If it is someone from your past, put down their name, the age you were when you were dealing with this person—for example, 21 to 23 years old. Then, write down all the things they did to you that hurt you. Then, write down the situation that occurred that made you say 'enough.' If you had the

courage to leave, I say congratulations and I hope you are in a better situation.

Remember that list so that you do not fall into a toxic relationship like that again. But, if this is still your current situation, write down the name of the person, the age you started dealing with this person, the things that hurt you, and then the things that you deserve - the way you should be talked to and loved. I guarantee you that you do not have to stay in a bad situation. There is courage deep down inside of you to make a new start. Believe that God will not leave you when you need him the most. Be safe, be smart, love yourself, and take care of yourself - especially if you have a child or children because they are depending on you.

CHAPTER 4
LOVE SHOULDN'T HURT LIKE THIS

I started dating a year after I broke up with Queens. I made sure I took time to heal so that I would not carry any baggage into my next relationship.

"Hello," a nice-looking man said as I arrived at my car after leaving a birthday party. "Hello," I replied. We had a short conversation and exchanged numbers. I called him Country Boy because he was from Georgia.

At our first dinner, we had a great time and then went to the movies. We spent a lot of time on the phone together.

He said "I am separated. Things did not work out between her and I. We decided to separate at the end of her second pregnancy. But we have two beautiful children. The divorce is almost final, but the state of Virginia has a waiting period and that period is almost up."

I met his ex-very briefly. She said hi and walked away. I would see her when we would pick up the kids from her. The kids were two years old and eight months old. They were at my house a lot because, after dating for five months, we moved in together. I know now that was way too fast. I would not advise that to anyone, especially if you have a child.

Country Boy could fix anything. I was just ready to buy a new vacuum cleaner because mine was broken, but he took it apart and fixed it. He fixed my computer when it was not working, too. He did everything around the house that I needed to be fixed. He would figure it out and just fix it. A different kind of fixing, but he even used to fix my meals for lunch when I went to work, and he would make sure the kids were taken care of.

Country Boy worked in the daytime and I worked three days a week so that helped us have a good amount of family time. The great thing about his job was that after the work was done, he could go home no matter what time it was. This gave us even more time together. And, he played for a minor football league in the area and invited me to all his games.

Finally, I had the relationship I deserved. Country Boy was responsible with the kids, he was responsible with the finances, he even helped me clear the jewelry credit card off my credit report, and he helped me pay all the bills. Things were going great until I started working labor and delivery. The workload was so demanding, I could not chart my work into the computer until after I gave report to the oncoming nurse, which was 6:45 p.m. That's the only time I was not being shuffled back and forth from one emergency to the next. This caused me not to get home sometimes until 9:30 p.m. at night.

Country Boy thought I was cheating on him because now, suddenly, I was getting home late. I tried to explain it to him that I am working on a different unit now that requires different charting and a heavier workload. He just did not get it and packed up all his things and left.

Late the next night, I'm home on the phone with Landy, and I hear my doorbell ringing over and over and over. I also hear some fast, loud knocking. I tell my friend on the phone to hold on and I look through the peephole. Country Boy is standing there on the other side of the door.

"It's him," I told my friend on the other line. "I'll call you back." As I cracked the door, I started to say, "I don't want to argue." But right after I got the word 'don't' out, he pushed the door all the way open, grabbed me by neck, and pushed me to the floor. He closed the door behind him.

I was in shock. I hit the tile floor pretty hard. My house phone started ringing in the kitchen. He then grabbed me by my hair and drug me down the hallway into the kitchen. He made me answer the phone because he thought it was another man, but in fact it was my friend calling back because she did not hear me tell her I would call her back. She just thought I had hung up. I told her I would call her back and tried to make my voice sound like everything was okay. After I hung up the phone, he dragged me upstairs and we began to wrestle.

"I don't want to be with you! You need to leave!" After a while, he did. He called the next day and apologized.

He said "I never done anything like that before and I'll never do it again. I never been in love like this before. I just thought you were cheating on me, but that's not how I am or have ever been."

I still did not take him back. I did miss his kids and my son missed him and the kids, too. But I just could not do it. After two months of no calls or pop-ups went by, someone told me that they saw him in the ER with a girl and his two children. So, I went up there and it was not his children's mother.

"Mommy! Mommy!" his kids yelled when they saw me and ran up to me to give me a hug. My motherly instincts kicked in and I just picked them up.

"I don't know who that chick is, but the children are going with me and you can pick them up from my house."

He followed me out to the car and put the car seats in my car and I drove them home. Biologically, they were not mine, but I loved them, and I just did not feel like that was a good situation where he had them. After an hour, Country Boy came by the house and I already had given the kids dinner and a bath. They were asleep and he and I had a talk.

"I'm sorry I didn't believe you about your job. I want to come back. All that arguing and fighting is not gonna happen no more. I want us to work it out." Needless to say, we also had to address the elephant in the room.

"But who was that random chick you were sitting with in the ER?"

"She was just a friend who got sick and needed a ride to the ER."

But I am thinking "Okay, that's fine, but you don't have to sit there and wait with the kids with her in the ER. That's a bit much if y'all are just friends."

"There is nothing going on between us," he insisted.

I took him back. We ended up working things out and were doing really good. Our relationship was loving and fun. The kids were really happy. We moved on with our lives together. One day, while we were watching an NFL football game, Country Boy started making hot wings in the kitchen. I love watching sports - football, basketball, or soccer. It does not matter. I was so into the game, and then I hear him start yelling something from the kitchen.

"No, no. Don't fry my wings hard," I say not really knowing what he was yelling about.

"The kitchen is on fire!" he screamed, but I am still not hearing him. When the football game went to commercial, I started to really focus on what he was saying.

"The kitchen is on fire!" he yelled again. I jumped up to run into the kitchen, and everything on my lap went flying left and right. The pot was in flames, so I grabbed the fire extinguisher and opened the back door to the kitchen. He threw the pan outside, sprayed the kitchen with the fire extinguisher, and then sprayed the pan outside. We put the fire out, and after everything was said and done, we just laughed.

"All you could think about was food. You couldn't even hear what I was saying. You were so focused on getting your food cooked the way you like it", he laughed. We laughed for a few minutes more because I knew it was true. I get upset if my food doesn't come out right. Good thing none of the kids were in the house and it was just us two.

On my birthday, he proposed to me. He tricked me, because I had asked for a camcorder. Although I unwrapped a camcorder box, I knew it was not heavy enough to have a camcorder inside.

"There ain't no camcorder in here," I said confused.
"Look deeper," he said from behind me.
"But I don't see anything. Where?" I said.

"Just keep looking," he said. And, as I swiveled around and showed him the inside of the empty box, I saw he had knelt down on one knee, and had a ring in his hand.

"Will you do me the honor of being my wife?" he asked. My mother was there, too.

"Yes, of course I will," I responded with all my heart. I said yes because we had truly worked through our past issues.

Country Boy wanted to move to Virginia Beach, so he applied for some jobs there and received many offers. But the money was not good enough. One job offered him the position, but not the salary advertised. So, the New Yorker in me had to show him how to negotiate.

"I won't accept anything less than four over what was advertised," he said when he called the company with me standing there behind him, coaching him on.

"Tell them to re-review your resume, and that you are more than qualified for the position," I whispered by his side. So, the company did just that and gave him the salary he asked for.

We soon moved to a townhouse in Virginia Beach that Country Boy had purchased, but I was the one who negotiated the price. We got it for way below the asking price. The New Yorker in me, I just did not see us paying the price everyone else pays. Once we finally moved, Country Boy wanted me to change jobs, and eventually I did, because the drive was starting to get dangerous after having worked a 12-hour shift.

I tried working Monday through Friday doing an office job with a little bit of fieldwork, but I did not enjoy the office part. I am a hands-on kind of person, so the fieldwork part of the job of going into homes and meeting new clients, or supervising other nurses doing their jobs, were the best parts of the job.

One morning, I rushed to a client's house and I had not had the chance to eat breakfast. When I got there, I taught her how to inject herself with her medication and other things. Then, I began to feel dizzy, light-headed, and nauseous. I finished up with her and thought it was just really hot in the house because you know how people love to keep their houses on 80+ degrees. But, after I got to my car, I called my supervisor to say I was going to Urgent Care because I really was not feeling well. Then, I thought, 'Well maybe I'm not feeling well because I hadn't eaten.'

But I was pregnant! Country Boy was more excited than I had ever seen him. For the next three months, I was very sick with nausea and vomiting. I had to call out of work often. My job let me go because I missed too many hours. This was the first time in my life that I had ever been let go and it sucked, because I already had my two-year-old son and Country Boy's two-year-old and one-year-old children at home - three toddlers and one on the way. After a few weeks, the sickness had gone, and I started applying for different jobs.

Arguments with Country Boy started up again, getting worse and worse, until the shoving started. Then, he would slap me if I said something he did not like, or he would grab me by my neck and start choking me. He started staying out late and coming home from work late.

While I was applying for jobs, God seemed to lead me back to the area where we used to stay. I don't know why I went over there, but it was familiar to me. So, I guess there was a level of comfort there, where I felt I could clear my head and process all that was happening to me.

Am I the type of woman to let a man put his hands on me? No, I had to tell myself. I am not the type of woman to stay in an abusive relationship. But, here I am. Before heading back home through the tunnel, I stopped at Walmart and as I was standing in line I bumped into my former co-worker, Cathy, from a previous hospital.

"You should cross into the blue," she suggested. This meant a contractor nurse position at the Air Force Base was available. I applied that night. I did not care that it would be a 45-minute drive each way. When I applied for the position, unfortunately, they only had a PRN position available at the time, which meant a nurse position only when needed. I just wanted to get my foot in the door. So, I interviewed for the position anyway. The interview went so well that they offered me a full-time position. That was better news than finding out I was pregnant.

"Thank you, God, Thank you God," I immediately started praying and crying out loud when I got off the phone. My prayers were being answered. I can be independent! Depending on Country Boy had me vulnerable. It had me accepting some of the things he did because I was not in a position where I could provide for myself and my son on my own.

I did not tell the agency, nor the supervisor, that I was pregnant, because I was afraid, they wouldn't hire me, and especially because I knew that I could do the job. All my credentials were verified, and my background check and drug test were cleared to work on base. I was 17 weeks pregnant on the first day of work. I saw Cathy again, the one who told me to cross into the blue. She worked the night shift and was about to go home. I was just coming on to start day shift orientation for the unit.

"Are you okay?" she asked me, noticing I was not feeling well.
"Oh, I'm just having some cramping. I'm gonna take something after breakfast." The truth was that the night before, Country Boy had really lost his temper. He did not like that I was going back to work on that side of town. He punched me a few times in the side of my stomach. All I could do was get down to protect my unborn fetus.

That morning, I met my preceptor, Angela, who took me on a tour of the unit. I met the staff and I also met Traci and Naomi who were also on night shift with Cathy. Everyone seemed so friendly. I familiarized myself with the unit. Angela then took me to tour the nursery. The cramping got so bad that I felt short of breath.

"Are you okay?" Angela stopped and asked. She had seen something that I had not noticed yet. Fluid was coming down my leg and then, just after she asked, a bigger gush of warm fluid came pouring out, soaking through my scrub pants, and splashing onto the floor.
I immediately ran to the locker room and into the bathroom.

"Are you pregnant? "Angela asked after following me into the locker room. "How many weeks?" she asked, and I told her I was17 weeks. Angela gave me a bunch of towels to dry off. I was completely drenched. "We need to get to one of the labor rooms", she said.

"I'll just stay in the bathroom," I said embarrassed.

"That is not an option. If you don't come out of there, your supervisor will be coming in to get you." I finally came out of the bathroom and started walking towards the labor room. The supervisor was on her way towards me just as I was coming out. I took up the last labor bed, so they had to close the unit until someone delivered. My preceptor was now my labor nurse.

"Your water has broken," the doctor confirmed after examining me. I was in pre-term labor. The baby had a heartbeat but would not be able to survive once it came out. I was too early in the pregnancy. I called Country Boy, my sister, and my parents, and told them what was happening. They all came up there and were supportive. You could not even tell that Country Boy had anger issues. He was holding my hand, rubbing my back, and being so concerned and attentive. He was sad because, despite his abusive behavior, he did want another baby.

They had to start Pitocin on me to induce the labor because I needed to deliver the fetus, and because I was now at an increased risk of infection since my water had already broken.

Hours later, I felt I had to pee, so I stood up, and when I did, I felt pressure, so I jumped back into the bed and the baby came out just like that. The doctor came in the room and clamped and cut the umbilical cord and told me that the baby had a heartbeat but that it would eventually stop. The nurse wrapped the baby up and gave him to me. I was still in shock and I did not cry because I was in disbelief.

Country Boy held the baby for a while and then put him on the warmer. The doctor was having difficulty getting the afterbirth of the placenta out.

An hour had gone by and the placenta still would not come out. Then, the night shift started coming back in to work.

Traci and Naomi, the nurses I had met earlier, ended up getting me ready for the OR (Operating Room) because the doctor had to use a machine to get the afterbirth out. They explained that anesthesia would put me to sleep during the procedure. The procedure should have only taken less than 40 minutes but instead, took two hours. I lost one liter of blood, but I made it through. When I woke up, I was back on the unit floor and Cathy was my nurse. I was connected to an IV that was on a pole and when we got to the bathroom, I felt really weak, so she had to assist me.

Now, here's the dilemma. In African American culture, we are taught from a young age that we do not sit on public toilets, and Cathy knew this, because we had a long conversation about this before. She told me that little girls were not taught this in White culture. But, as weak as I was, I could not squat. So, I was going to have to try something new.

"Nicole, I cleaned it myself!" she said proudly when she saw my hesitant face. So, I sat down and went to the bathroom.

"Cathy, I'm about to go," I said, meaning I was about to pass out. I had sudden tunnel vision and I became short of breath and lightheaded. Cathy rushed me back to the bed. She took my blood pressure and it was 70/30. I passed out soon thereafter. When I came to, Country Boy was there by my side, and stayed there all night and went to work in the morning.

"Your blood count is low from the blood lost during the afterbirth procedure. You need a blood transfusion," the doctor told me.

"That doesn't sound good to me doctor," I said. I cannot say why, but I was scared to get the transfusion. So instead, the doctor had me take iron pills three times a day. Mom made me her famous liver and onions. And, I ate spinach, collard greens, and dark leafy salads three times a day. Finally, they discharged me after several days. It was not until I reached the parking lot that it hit me; I had lost my baby. I broke down and cried so hard on the spot. Country Boy had to carry me to the car, where I continued to cry. Words cannot express the pain a woman feels when she loses a child, even though my baby never made it past a few minutes out of the womb. It was a deep grief.

I went back to work after a week. I did not want to lose this job. Everyone was really kind when I went back, and it was only awkward for the first two shifts, and then everyone was at ease. Things at home, well that's another story. A month after the loss, Country Boy wanted to try again to get pregnant. I was not ready, but I did not want to argue and fight. He started coming home late again and so one day I called up his friend's wife. "I need to get out of the house. Let's go grab something to eat," I told her.

Country Boy came home as I was leaving and told me to take his car because he had a nice rental at the time, as someone had hit his car, and it was in the shop. I thought nothing of it and took his car to pick up Zee. We went to the Roger Brown's Restaurant and talked. Zee said hello to a guy passing by and he stopped to start a conversation. Then, he called his brother, VA, over. VA and I started talking about real estate. He said he was a real estate appraiser and I asked him for his card because my fiancé and I were just starting to flip houses, and we could use his services. After the conversation, they walked us to our car because it was late and, back then, it was not the safest parking garage to be in late at night. Zee opened the back door to put her food on the seat when she saw something there. "Shut up," Zee whispered.

"Who are you talking to?" I asked her as she caught me off guard.

"Shhhhhh," she whispered again and simultaneously pulled out a tape recorder. Apparently, Country Boy had slipped a voice activated tape recorder onto the backseat. "Who in the world are you engaged to?" VA said in disbelief.

I was so embarrassed. Me and Zee just said good night to the guys, jumped in the car, and left. We listened to the recording and heard our conversations, which was regular girl talk, but I just could not believe the nerve of him. He was trying to catch me cheating. But, as I said before, I do not cheat. I confronted him immediately about the tape recorder. He told me he had been using that on me for a while but never found anything. That is because I was not doing anything.

Later, he started talking about buying a house back in the area that I used to live in so that I could be closer to work. I was able to find a house out there for us and, while having a second look at the house together, I remembered being in the car praying that God would take this unhealthy relationship away from me, and then seeing Cathy who told me about the job.

"You know", I started saying as I turned towards Country Boy while he was driving. "You know how sometimes people just continue to be together because it's what's expected? I feel if people are unhappy, they should tell the other person and then they should just go their separate ways and take a break."

"We should take a break," he agreed. I immediately began to cry, first, because God heard me and, second, I was sad because I did love him, but knew he was not good for me. I immediately knew that he was cheating. He moved out the next day. I was no fool. I know he was going so he could move in with another woman. He swore up and down that there was no one else, but my gut knew the truth.

A few days later, I was in the store with my sister's friend and my phone rang with his number. "Hello?" I say, but then I hear a woman's voice in the background.

"Hi, baby. Give me a hug," she was talking in the background. So, I hung up the phone. "You're a cheater and a liar," I called back to say and then hung up again.

I moved my son and I back to the old house until the new house was ready. Country Boy came over and tried to talk to me. All this should not have mattered since I wanted to break up with him anyway, but I was disgusted. I do take responsibility, however. I stayed in that relationship way too long. But again, on the bright side of things, I was looking forward to starting fresh, waiting to close on my first house. Ironically, Country Boy's ex-wife ended up being my realtor. This was the first time we ever got to sit down and talk, and she actually apologized to me.

"Country Boy and I were still married, not separated, when you and him started a relationship. He just recently told me how he lied to you about being separated. I'm so sorry for not liking you in the beginning, but that's the reason why. I didn't know that you didn't know our relationship was not really over. Thank you for taking such great care of my children and treating them well. He even said he was planning on leaving me after I had already bought another house for him to flip."

Country Boy thinks he is slick, but he does not know the God I serve, because the God I serve made sure nothing that I purchased was in his name. But, then, a problem occurred with closing on the new house. When the contractor was fixing some things in the house, he forgot to put the key back in the lock box, so that when the appraiser came, he could not get in to appraise the house. That was a problem because you have only a certain amount of days to have everything done in order for the deal to go through. Otherwise, you have to start all over again.

My realtor told me the only way to get this done is to see if someone else can come out and appraise the house. Right then, God reminded me of VA. I still had VA's card in my wallet. I immediately called him.

"Hey VA. Do you remember me? I met you and your brother at that restaurant five months ago".

"I think you meant to call someone else," VA said.
"You don't remember the woman with the tape recorder in the car?" I asked.
"Oh! That's you?! Yeah, I can't forget that story!" he said and we both started laughing.

"Would you be able to come and do an appraisal? I broke up with my fiancé and I need to get this house appraised within the next three days so I can move in", I said. "Sure. I can come out tomorrow," he said.

My realtor and I met VA at the property, and he appraised the house. It went straight back to the office, the paperwork got done, and then it was all sent over to the mortgage broker the day after that. Everything was done and approved. I was so thankful to Jesus because now I was a homeowner. Yes, this little project girl was a homeowner. Thanks to God.

VA and I kept in contact. He called me right before I went in to sign my mortgage. He was actually the first person I called when I got out from signing. "Congratulations!" he told me. "We need to celebrate such a big occasion! Can I take you to lunch or dinner?"

"Absolutely."

He was very nice, tall, and in great shape, and he could make me laugh. He even helped me move some things out of my old house with Country Boy. I was nervous going there but once VA said he would go with me; all my nervousness went away. VA also helped me move my stuff from storage into my new house. He would see when I was down and deep in thought about Country Boy and get my mind off him by making me laugh.

Laughter is definitely good for the soul and VA started becoming good for my soul. We became close quickly. I could not believe that someone could hold me so tight when I was crying so hard over another man. My friend, Landy, told me one day to stop crying over Country Boy. "Later down the line you gonna be mad at yourself for crying over him for so long," Landy insisted. Country Boy left a lot of pain and hurt that I had to pray to God to take away.

VA told me that he had done a few appraisals for Country Boy's ex-wife. He told me that Country Boy married the woman he cheated on me with

TAKE IT BACK

and bought her a really nice ring and a big ole house in Chesapeake, Virginia. VA knew because he had appraised the house. Country Boy bought a brand-new Ford Expedition with rims and bought his wife a brand-new Nissan Altima. He cheated on me, and now he's doing really good? This was not good news to me. I wanted revenge, but I decided to trust God instead.

But then, I heard that Country Boy started making bad deals and that his tenants started missing rental payments on five of his seven properties. He started owing lots of people money and not just the banks. Him, his ex-wife, the new wife, and the kids, picked up and left for Louisiana. They had bought a dump truck and went down to make money doing cleanup for Katrina. It was good for a while, but then their truck started breaking down and they were on food stamps, living in a two-bedroom apartment. His ex-wife and kids left and moved back with family.

Then, he got word that his big ole house in Chesapeake was getting foreclosed. So, he drove up in the Expedition to quickly get things out of the house, and while he was there packing up the U-Haul and the Expedition, the Repo Man was watching and repo-ed the truck right while he was in the house. The Repo Man was looking to repossess the wife's car, too, but that was still back in New Orleans.

This information was given to me by a mutual friend of his and mine, and the day I heard that, all the pain and hurt went away. God handled it. I actually felt sorry for him, because at least I had my faith in God to take me through my ups and downs. Country Boy did not all the way believe in God. He had a lot of childhood issues.

CHAPTER 5
HOUSE TO HOUSE

VA and I developed a friendship and had a lot of lunches and dinners together, because my schedule was flexible, given the days and nights that I worked. One evening, VA called me, and he sounded like he could not breathe. "I need to come over and talk," he said. So, I called out of the work madness and waited for him to come over.

The lost stare on his face showed me such extreme sadness. "My mother just passed away from cancer." What could I say? We just sat down on my couch silently until he began to cry. He wept so hard, and loudly. I had never heard this kind of distress from a man. I just hugged him tight until he fell asleep from exhaustion from the pain he was going through. VA had been there for me when I was crying over Country Boy and, that night, I told myself, it was my turn to be there for him.

This is really how our friendship became a relationship. We saw each other in our most vulnerable moments, and we were there for each other. His sadness over his mother made me feel so dumb and so mad about ever crying over Country Boy. Landy was right! VA and I would go out together with our friends and one time he invited me to his brother's birthday party at a club. It was a nice summer's night and I wore an all-white, shear halter top. It was classy, not trashy. I had on white capris and white stiletto heels, too, with my accessories sparkling. I got a lot of eager looks that night, but no one could even get close to me because VA was stuck at my side.

They played Kanye West's "Gold Digger" song that had just come out - but no I am not a gold digger. VA sure was not broke, however. He had a great career. He was a six-figure thoroughbred, with a chiseled and sculpted body. We would always try to out-dance each other everywhere we went where there was music. Yes, I was way happier in this relationship. He got along with all my friends and co-workers. We had game nights and went to game nights. We spent time with my son and took him to the park. He played football with my son. We just really enjoyed each other.

A year later, I became pregnant. VA was so excited. He asked Landy to be the godmother. The pregnancy was going well. I did not tell anyone at work because of the previous miscarriage. I wanted to wait until I was further along. But, at 17 weeks, a phone call from the doctor put a jolt on the progress. "We are looking at the ultrasound and something might be wrong with the placement of the placenta. You must immediately go on bed rest."

"For how long?"
"A few months."
"What? How can I provide for my son? How will I pay my bills?"

Thankfully, however, I was cleared after a few more ultrasounds. I could not imagine being out of work. I loved my job as an L&D nurse, but most of all, I loved my co-workers, because they were a second family to me. Also, I had been working since I was 15 years old. So, I do not know what it is like not to work. I was way too young not to work.

When I told everyone at work that I was six months pregnant, they were in shock. I had hidden it for so long, right up under their noses, just in case anything went wrong again. It is really hard after a miscarriage. People do not know what to say and if someone else is expecting, that person feels as if they cannot be happy around you. It is a very sensitive time.

But this time was different. I was further along in the pregnancy, just past the age of viability of 24 weeks. So, if the baby was to be born right now, there was a higher chance they would be able to save the baby's life. Everything was blissful throughout my pregnancy. VA made it to all my appointments. We had two baby showers, one in Virginia with work family and my immediate family, and one in New York. Even Queen's mother showed up and was excited for us. She considered this her grandbaby too. Things could not have been more perfect, and then VA dropped a bomb on me when I was eight months pregnant.

He was still married, and he did not tell his wife about me being pregnant. VA assured me they were separated, but that she just did not know he was going to be a father again. "You need to tell her," I said. And, he told her. Then, I get a phone call from her saying that . . . they had never been separated!!!! My heart dropped. Again, betrayed. "But I forgive him. I still want to be with my husband," the wife told me next. "I have no plans or intentions of raising this baby by myself," I came back and we both just sat there quietly on the phone. As soon as we hung up, I called VA and yelled at him for lying to me. Could this really be happening to me . . . again?

A week before my due date, around lunch time, I called him and told him I was having mild contractions and to stay close to his phone. I had actually called him the night before to say that the contractions were getting stronger - no answer. I called again this time and then again after a few minutes - still no answer. The contractions later slowed down and weakened, so I went to sleep.

The next morning, he called and called, but my feelings were hurt, because if I had gone into labor, I would have been doing it without him since he was not reachable. I ignored his calls all that morning and afternoon. When I finally picked up in the afternoon, he acted like he was so concerned that I had already had the baby. "My wife and I had been calling around to all the hospitals in the area to see if you were there." Are you kidding me? He was with her last night.

Everything was crashing again. How could he hurt me when he knew what I had just been through? How could he lie? How could he be this selfish? Better yet, how could I be so blind? How could I tell my family? VA came over so we could talk.

"I am confused. I want to be with you, but I also want to be there for my son that I had with my wife. I am still going through with the divorce. When I'm over there, I'm just spending time with my son."

Fast forward, my water broke exactly the morning of my due date. Being an L&D nurse, or actually anyone in OB (Obstetrics) can tell you, it is really rare to have the baby on your actual due date. The night before I was at my sister's house watching the movie *What's Love Got To Do With It*. When Angela Bassett, acting as Tina Turner, sang "Rolling on the River," I danced the whole routine, big belly and all, kick turns and everything. After that, I went shopping at Walmart at about 10:00 that night, just grabbing little last-minute things. I was nesting again, full of energy the day before I would birth my child, but, again, I did not realize it. I probably danced myself into labor, because around 1:30 in the morning, I felt a big contraction that was so strong, it woke me straight up out of bed. Then, I heard a pop. I jumped out the bed and water began running down my leg.

'My water is breaking and it's just me and my five-year-old son at home', I said to myself. I called VA's phone twice, back-to-back, but no answer. So, I had no choice but to call his house phone, and his wife picked up. She woke him up and told him that my water broke. I heard him say okay and that he was on his way. He called me when he got in his car.

"Wait for me to get to you," he said. So, I took a shower and all the while the contractions were getting worse. It is a 45-minute drive from where he was to my house. I got out the shower and got dressed. I threw on some maternity capris, some wedges, and a tank top because it was summertime and just because you are pregnant, it does not mean you cannot dress up and look cute. I had just gotten my hair done two days before. "Wake up and get dressed," I said to my son. We were both ready when VA pulled up. It was raining outside, and VA was very nervous. He was so focused trying to keep the umbrella over my head that the truck door kept closing every time he tried to open it for me to get in, because the truck was parked in the driveway on an incline. The contractions were so strong that I started swatting the umbrella out of VA's hand and fussing at him to hold the door open so I could get into the back. I climb in the back seat and get on my hands and knees. I call my sister and tell her I am having a baby and to meet me at the hospital. My sister missed my first child's delivery by an hour, so I really wanted to make sure she was there this time. I called my Mom and Dad as well.

I held onto VA's arm and dug my nails into his skin, squeezing it from the back seat. He tried to take my hand off his arm and put it on the armrest of the passenger seat. But I just put it right back because of all the pain I was in. You have the audacity to be thinking your arm is hurting? I wish you could feel what I'm feeling instead.

I was not thinking about a seatbelt either. All I wanted to do was get to the hospital and get my epidural. I was still on my hands and knees in the backseat of the truck when I felt us get off at an exit. Although I could not see where we were going, I knew it was too soon to be exiting because the curve into the correct exit did not feel like this. I knew this because my son's school was off the same exit as the hospital, and I drove him there five times a week. This curve was taking too long. "What exit did we just get off at?"

"I got it, I got it," he protested, but when I picked my head up to see, it was the wrong exit.
"Make-a-U-turn-at-the-light!" I barked at him with my mouth tight.

"No, I got it. The hospital is right here," he said. But then he realized he got off at the wrong exit. He quickly made a sharp U-turn, which then had me going forward because I was not buckled in. So, he reaches back to help me, while he was getting thrown into the door himself.

We got back onto the highway and off at the right exit. We pulled up to the hospital, and it just so happened there was a nurse standing outside the hospital smoking a cigarette. She was able to quickly let us in with her badge. VA swung the car door open, got me out, and then my son unbuckled his seatbelt and got out as well. VA tried to grab a wheelchair for me as we were entering the hospital doors, but I was making a beeline for the elevators. They were both running behind me with the wheelchair, trying to get me to sit down, but it was just so much pressure that I could not sit down. We got into the elevator and there were only about three other people in the elevator who were not pregnant. I held onto VA's neck moaning and breathing through the contractions.

The other people in the elevator were scared I was going to have the baby right there in the elevator. We got onto the labor and delivery unit and the nurses were sitting behind the desk.

"Can I help you?"

"Yes, I'm having this baby right now," I heaved out.

"Oh, what's your name? Your social security number? What's your date of birth?"

I know they have to ask that stuff, but they did not understand that I wanted my epidural. The contractions were getting stronger. It was 3:30 a.m. by this time. But I was in my cute outfit still. So, maybe they did not realize that I was really going to have a baby?

There were three beds in the triage room, and you could pull the curtains in between each bed to give the patient privacy. Thank God I was the only one in triage then. A girl came that I did not know, and I do not know if she was a CNA (certified nursing assistant) or a new nurse or what. "I need you to pee in a cup." She stated.

"I cannot pee because this baby is coming right now, and if I push anything out of myself, the baby is going to drop right here." The triage nurse, Jenny, came and rescued me thankfully. "Okay love. Come on. Get in bed. Let me put you on the monitor and check you." "Umm, baby? I left the truck running in front of the hospital," VA says. In front of this hospital? You do not leave a running SUV Limited Edition with the keys in the ignition and the windows down in front of this hospital.

"Go get my truck and park it! You better hurry up!" I exclaimed. He and my son, who was five at the time, rushed downstairs to move the car.

Meanwhile, the nurse put me on a monitor to check me. I was ten centimeters already and ready to push the baby out.

"Nooooo!"

"What's the matter?"

"I wanted an epidural," came out in a whiny voice. As soon as I said this, the next contraction hit, and I had to push.

"No, no. Don't do that love," Jenny said, and then she started calling out for people. She called for NICU, pediatricians, and OB doctors. NICU is the Newborn Intensive Care Unit. A resident came and the triage nurse said this is Dr. So-and-So and she's going to deliver your baby.

"No, you're going to deliver my baby," I turned my head to the triage nurse to say. I knew that she knew what she was doing and had been doing it for a very long time. I was on the second push when VA and my son came back into the room. My son saw his little brother's head poking out of my lady parts.

"Cover his eyes," I said. I did not want him to see anything like that at five-years old. I did not know if he was going to be grossed out or freaked out. But then I pushed one more time, and my second son was born.

Even though I was not screaming during the birth, the pain was so traumatic. There was no crying from me when he came out. I could only focus on the ring of fire, that was the stretching of my vagina, when the baby's head was coming out. It was soul-shaking. Imagine that time when you were a little kid and the Ringling Brothers put gasoline on that big ole ring, lit it, and then the fire starts in one spot and quickly goes around the whole circle. That is exactly the feeling like someone pouring gasoline on my vagina, lighting it up, and a fire going around it, engulfing it in flames.

They cut the umbilical cord and then asked me if I wanted to hold the baby and feed him. I was so traumatized that I told them to give him to his father. "Selfish," VA called me. I was thankful that my son was healthy and sounding good, but my vagina was still on fire and I just could not get past the initial shock.

"Two Percocet, please," I said immediately to my doctor when he walked into the room. "No problem. You earned it!" he quickly replied.

Mom, Dad, and my sister entered next. They had just missed the delivery by five minutes. My sister was so disappointed. She missed another delivery by her only sister. VA stayed until 9 o'clock in the morning and then he went into work. He knew I had a plethora of friends coming to visit me throughout the day, and I would mostly need him in the nighttime. After so many visitors, I felt overwhelmed with love, but I also had not had much rest. I was so happy, however, when my son's godmother, Landy, came. When I saw her, I breastfed my son and finally fell asleep, the best two hours of sleep I've had all day. Rest and hydration are best after having a baby so you can keep your milk supply up. Later, VA came in and bought me some food and my son's God Mom left.

"My wife wants to come up to the hospital and see the baby," VA said. Okay, here we go back into the twilight zone. I mean, who does that? Aren't you legally separated just waiting for the divorce papers to be signed because the law says you have to wait a year and now your wife wants to come and visit my baby? And, to see me of all people, who technically cheated on her with you?

"No, she cannot come up to the hospital, because my family doesn't know any of the story. It would not be good, especially if my sister found out that you lied to me and have a whole wife," I immediately said. "My sister is very overprotective of me." So, his wife never came up and he spent both nights with me in the hospital.

On the day of discharge, VA came and got me and took me and his son home to my house. He stayed for the first five days and then he told me he would be back, that he was going to see his other son. He told me that he wanted to be with me and that he was going to go through with his divorce. My son was about a week old and I just sat and listened, having another good gut feeling about what VA was saying. I later called his wife and told her what he had been telling me.

"He's been telling me he wants our marriage to work, and that he just needs time with you to tell you but that he didn't want to tell you right now because you just had his baby. He didn't want you to have postpartum depression," she went on. "We all need to sit down in front of each other so that he can't tell anymore lies", I responded.

"I agree," the wife said. "Come over. He's here."

I drove 45 minutes to Portsmouth and parked in the driveway and rang the doorbell with my seven-day-old infant with me. My five-year-old was up in New York with one of his grandmothers that I dearly loved. VA answered the door and had no idea I was coming but that his wife knew it. "Why are you here?" he asked as he let me in.

"Because we all need to talk."
"Oh, well y'all can talk. I'm good."

"What do you want to do? Are you gonna make your marriage work or are you gonna' be with me?" his wife asked.

He would not answer the question, and I just got up and went into the bathroom and started crying my emotions out all over the place.
I had not been eating or sleeping and when I'm not eating, you know that's bad. This is not what I had envisioned. VA came into the bathroom and when he saw I was crying, knelt and started wiping my tears.

Later, his wife would tell me that when she saw this, she knew he was in love with me because he would never have done that for her. She said she would cry, and he would just get annoyed, but, with me, he was compassionate. I took my newborn and went home. I had some tough decisions to make and I was not ready, or in a good state of mind, to make them. After a few more weeks, VA came to work things out with me. He wanted to move on with his life with me. I was really happy because I did not want to raise my newborn and other son by myself. And, I really loved VA.

When my son reached ten months, VA was laid off from his job. I went and got another job part-time doing L&D, in addition to my full-time L&D job. It was very hard because it seemed like I was not spending time with my children and I was constantly at work. VA got depressed about not having a job and he would not help keep the house clean. He would sit at home all day long until it was time to get the boys from daycare and school and then he would make sure the boys ate. But he would wait until I got home and then would ask me what I was going to prepare for him to eat.

Money was tight, but we had groceries. Still he would ask to eat out when I got home or have me scramble to try to figure out what me and him was going to eat. I had two jobs. I did not feel like cooking, nor did I feel like the cooking responsibility was mine. If the roles had been reversed and I was not working, he would have expected the house to at least be clean since I would be home all day.

He picked up a hobby of flag football and I would give him my debit card for gas money. But he would use more money than he was supposed to, and then we would not have enough money for the bills sometimes. I was so fed up. I called his father and his father told me to take my card away from his son. So, I did. I always want to help whoever I am with. I do not want to see them doing badly. If I can help, I wanna help. But this was way more than I could handle.

Then, VA's car broke down and would not run, so my mother let him use her car, not knowing everything he had done. After seven months of being unemployed, VA got a seasonal job with UPS. This was a good start, although the pay was not enough after taxes. It covered gas and VA's personal items only. All the weight of paying all the bills was still on me. After the seasonal job was over, he got a job cleaning carpets and the same thing happened after taxes - it was not enough.

Then, VA started disappearing a lot, taking a lot of phone calls outside of the house. When I approached him about it, he called me paranoid. However, just a little while after that, I found out he was cheating again. Again, I tried to work through this kind of situation as I had done in the past. But he was still cheating, just after I had gotten over the first time. I was in a lot of credit card debt because I was paying all the bills myself. I was so frustrated, and we argued a lot, but never in front of the kids, and never in front of friends or family. Whatever issues we had, we always made sure we only argued alone.

A female that I suspected he was cheating with, kept calling his phone when we were home one day. The same number kept popping up. He always referred to her as a business connect because he was trying to get into music and become an artist's manager. A few days later, I sat him down near me and, unbeknownst to him, I answered the female's call so she could hear us talking.

"You are the only one that I love and the only one I'm with. I'm not seeing nobody else but you. I'm not sleeping with no one else but you. You are my whole world," he went on and on. She got to hear everything he said and then she hung up and called back. VA picked up the phone and I heard her yelling. "I thought you weren't with her anymore!?"

That's all I needed to hear. I knew he was up to his same tricks and I was not about to be part of his show any longer. I prayed and I cried, and I asked God to please take another one out of my heart so that I could leave again. I did not have the strength to walk away from VA on my own. I was laying across my kitchen table just crying. And, the next time he left out to a flag football game, I packed up all his clothes, because that's all he had, and put them in two big black garbage bags and left them in the garage. When he walked back through the door that night, I asked him could we talk. As we sat down on the couch and I was trying to gather up the words, I felt myself about to give him another chance, but he cut me off. "Go ahead and just say what you have to say," ended up being the first full sentence to come out of his mouth. He was so rude and abrupt.

"I don't want to be with you anymore," I went on.
"You need to leave," I said just like that.

I did not cry. I did not argue. I did not feel any heartache. I actually felt relief. He got up, went into the bathroom, and then he came back out and asked if he could take a shower first before he left, and I said yes. He acted like what I said had not affected him and then two minutes later he came back out from the bathroom and asked me if we could talk and if we could work things out. "No. You already showed me that you are not the one for me", I said. He begged for me to give him another chance and told me he would never cheat on me again.

But, this time, I did not take a man that I loved back. Tina Turner was ringing in my head, 'What's love got to do with it?' I finally had the strength not to fall back on a man's lies. I took my mother's car keys back from him and one of his friend's came to get him. VA ended up moving back in with his father.

VA would come and get our son for a few hours and then bring him back. On one of those visits, I had to work overtime and he stayed at the house with the boys. When I came home, he had cleaned my whole house, folded the laundry, mopped the floors, cleaned the bathrooms, and vacuumed. He even cooked! All the things I would have wanted him to. But this did not make me take him back.

One of his friends from Texas called him after a few months and told him he should come work out there doing pipe fitting and welding. I told VA he should try to go out there and become a safety manager because he had people skills and was good with paperwork. Of course, he did not listen and went out there just to make not enough money to be worth it. VA would borrow money from me while he was out in Texas because he only got paid the days he worked. If it rained, they did not work. I still had a soft spot in my heart for him and I imagined he could be a provider again. Maybe if this happened, he would not start cheating from feeling inadequate. I never thought he cheated because I was not doing what I was supposed to do. I always felt he cheated because he believed he did not match up to what I was giving the family, and not just financially, but all my hard work and always being such a caring person.

VA came home to visit his son once every six months, but when he was in Texas, he would go weeks without calling him. What I found out is that he was actually coming home every three months, but he would go and see his other son and his wife. He was telling the both of us the same lie that he was trying to keep things together so he could make everything up to us. After a while, it became months and months before he would pick up his phone when I called and then, if I asked him for money for his son, he would tell me he did not have it or that I should sue him for child support.

After three years of being in Texas, he finally took my advice and applied for the safety manager position and started making steady money. That is when I finally sued him for child support. The judge granted me $308 a month, not enough for a five-year-old who was in sports, after school programs, summer camp, and who needed a babysitter, with me working 12-hour night shifts. VA was so upset with me for filing and would not pay me back any of the money he borrowed from me when he was not working or when he needed me to supplement his income.

When he first got out to Texas, he made the excuse that when people are in relationships, they accrue certain expenses together. I told him we were never married and those were my loans to him. I am a single Mom. There is no way I was just giving someone money, especially a man.

Needless to say, I was celibate for three years after that last relationship. My friends and co-workers thought I had gone crazy, but I do not want to be sharing my body with anyone that I am not in a relationship with, not just anyone can get it. I am not a wait-until-marriage kind of woman either, because I want to know what I am getting myself into before I go and get married. I want it to be forever and I want to make sure that my husband is going to be everything that I need spiritually (equally yoked), physically, and emotionally. I know that is not the explanation that everyone can accept, but it is the realest answer I have to give. But, sexually, when the time is right, I do want to know what a man is working with. Sex is not everything, but that does not mean that it does not need to be good. I want to be fully compatible. I want forever to be forever!

CHAPTER 6
TIME STOPPED SO HERE COMES THE LETTER

Within the first few months of being celibate, I started teaching teenaged girls at Bible Study class at my church. I enjoyed it so much, especially because I love reading the Bible and I love going to Bible Study myself from time to time. The teenaged boys had their own instructor, but they would join my class, and after a while, we just grouped both together as Teenaged Bible Study. Teaching and learning from these kids were one of the best experiences of my life.

I was still a single mother raising two boys by myself but was able to be an example for young people and pour myself into their lives. After three years, my teenaged Bible Study kids graduated high school. New people took over the next group because I did not want to teach my one son's age group. I wanted him to hear lessons from someone else plus they had a male to teach and he needed male guidance. I just kind of kept up with the newly graduated teenagers.

After three years of being single and celibate, the new craze of online dating started, and my best friend, Annette, was on two different dating sites. So, I used to sit there and laugh at her because of some of the things people would say online. It was just so funny and so unbelievable. She got me to try Christian Mingle and I figured, why not? It would be nice to talk to somebody who at least I know believed in God and Jesus.

I did meet a very nice man, but he did not live close by. He lived almost four hours away. He also worked no less than 16-hour days, five times a week, and was a great father to two boys. We had great conversations and met up once for a day, but it never became anything more than a friendship. Neither one of us had any intention of moving to another state and I did not want to do any kind of long-distance relationship. He was probably the one that got away.

I tried another dating site, but there was no one with real conversation or substance on there. When you looked at a profile, even if you had not contacted the person, the person could still see when you visited their profile. So, I received a message from Philly one day. "I see you looked at my profile twice. Here is my number. Call me when you get a chance," he wrote.

I ended up calling him that evening while I was dropping my son off at an AAU basketball tournament and it just so happened Philly was there to coach a game for a different team. But I had just gotten back from vacation that day, so I did not stay, because I had my youngest son with me, and he wanted to go play at his friend's house. When the game was over, I picked my son up and we went back over to Annette's house because both the boys wanted to play with her son. While I was there, Philly called me and asked me if I was busy and could I come out and grab some dinner with him. Like I said many times before, I am a foodie. Obviously, the answer was yes, and the restaurant was really close to Annette's house—less than a five-minute drive.

I left the kids with Annette and went to dinner with Philly. I drove my own car there and I let my best friend know which restaurant I was at, texted her Philly's first and last name, and sent her a picture of him when I got there. People are so crazy these days that you have to take extra measures to make sure that you are safe. I took a chance with meeting people online because I really do not go out. The only time I go out, is out to eat. I do not go clubbing or go to a lot of other places. You will not even see me at fast-food restaurants, but you will see me dining in at restaurants because that is the one time when someone is asking me what I need instead of the other way around.

As a nurse, I am always catering to my patients and asking them and their family members what they need. Then, when I go home, I start asking my children what they need. Then, I turn to my man and ask him what he needs.

Me and Philly had a wonderful time at dinner. We talked. There was good conversation. Philly had one son and he was working full-time doing mechanical engineering. He volunteered to coach the kids' basketball team, which I felt was a really good quality in a man. The restaurant closed at 9 p.m. and we were the last two people in the restaurant just talking, eating, and sharing good humor until the restaurant staff had to tell us that they had to go home. We walked outside and into the parking lot just continuing with the conversation. After that, we talked on the phone a lot of times just getting to know each other.

One day, I went to work in the evening and Philly called me and asked me what to take for a toothache. I told him and he said he was going to go home, take the medicine, and get some sleep, because he had to work in the morning. That morning he calls me, and I was on my way home to put my son on the school bus. He asked me if I could come down to his job, pick him up, and take him to the doctor's. I hesitated because I had only known him three weeks. Plus, I just got off working a 12-hour shift. "Please, please, please", he kept saying. He told me he didn't have anyone else that could help him, and that his tooth hurts so bad, he wasn't going to be able to drive. I told him I would give him a call after I put my son on the school bus.

When I called him back, I told him to call the dentist and get an emergency appointment ahead of time. He gave me the address to his job and when I got there to pick him up, he looked terrible. He was in so much pain.

"Where is the dentist's office?" I asked him, when he got into the car.

"Oh, I did not call them yet", he replied.

"What? Call them now", I said. He called his insurance company who then called the dentist and found him an appointment within that next hour.

"What kind of health insurance do you have? I work for the government and they never did anything like that for me. I usually have to make my own appointments," I asked.

Then, I asked, "Are we going straight to your appointment or are you going to go home and shower?"

"Why do you ask me that?"

"Because you stink," I said matter of factly.

Philly smelled like metal, so we stopped at his house for a second to take a shower and change his clothes. I was leery about going into his house. I had only known him for three weeks and I am just funny-acting like that. I do not like being in an unknown environment and I did not want to be misunderstood as being there for any other reason than just for him to take a shower and get ready for me to take him to his dental appointment.

Whatever they did to his mouth at the dentist, made it swell up one side of his face like a chipmunk. He at least got a prescription for his toothache. I told him how to take the medicine and then I left and went home.

We spent more time together, after that, going to the movies and out to eat. He would cook for me, and all the time we spent talking on the phone just drew us closer together. I had knee surgery and he had to work that day, but that morning, before my surgery he prayed over me and it calmed me down. He said he would come see me after work. The surgery was scheduled to be an outpatient surgery, but when the surgeon started working on my knee, he was trying to get the pins in, and they would not connect. A one-hour surgery turned into a five-hour surgery and Annette, my best friend who was waiting in the waiting room, said she was about to come into the OR and find me because so many people had come in, had their surgeries, and left before me, even though I had gone in before them. No one came out to update her and she started pacing back and forth trying to figure out how to get into the OR.

After the surgery, when they brought me back to the recovery area, I would not wake up from the anesthesia, so they admitted me into the hospital. When I woke up and realized I had been in the hospital so long, I looked at Annette and asked what happened.
"Why am I here?" I asked.

"I already told you 27 times. Go to sleep and I'll tell you in the morning!" Annette snapped. I felt so sad. Why did she yell at me like that? Apparently, I had been coming in and out of consciousness, but each time I could not remember. She kept having to repeat herself so many times and she was over it. We still laugh about that to this day.

The next day I was able to go home, and I had to use crutches. I was only allowed to be on bed rest with bathroom privileges for the first three days. Philly came by after work and brought Annette and I some dinner. He took over for a few hours so she could take care of some things. I had on my robe when he was helping me up to go to the bathroom when my oldest son stepped in between us.

"I'll help my Mom to the bathroom," he said.

"Mom, I think he was looking at your butt," he whispered to me. Ha, ha, ha! I thought that was so cute that my son was being overprotective of me. In the beginning, my oldest son really did not like Philly, and I know it is because he just wanted it to be, he, his brother, and I. He did not want to share me with anyone else, especially now that he was older. My son wanted me to go back with his Dad. Philly could not understand it.

"How does he want you to be back with his father when he's never even seen y'all in a relationship together?" Philly asked.

"Kids always love their parents even when they do wrong. You're looking at it from adult eyes," I told Philly. "You're not looking at it through a kid's eyes. A kid always thinks there's a chance his parents will get back together." Meanwhile, my youngest son really liked Philly. He would go with me to visit Philly's family and he liked Philly's son, who was two when my son met him.

But then, adversity hit, and Philly got let go from his job. I felt sorry for him because it was plain to see he did a great job. His supervisor did not like him because he did not hold back his tongue when something was not right. Philly did not take the dismissal lightly. This sent him into the stages of grief. First, Philly was in shock that after ten years something like this could happen. I told him everything would be fine. I knew he would quickly find another job, but he told me that it would not be easy and that I could not understand because I was a nurse and in high demand everywhere.

He would not pick up my phone calls or answer the door if I came by to check on him. Second came anger. Philly got so irritated at the smallest things like even hearing someone say, 'good morning.' You could hear the frustration in almost every conversation. You could tell he was very anxious when he talked about how he was going to take care of his responsibilities. Third came bargaining. He was talking to old co-workers trying to tell his side of what happened. He was struggling to understand how they could sit by and allow his supervisor to make such a devastating decision just based on not liking an opinionated worker.

His depression set our relationship spiraling up and down like a roller coaster. Whenever he was coaching basketball, life was good. We visited his family members, and they had no clue of his situation. Anytime I brought up whether he had filed for unemployment, or looked for a job, he blew up. He talked about how the system is set against him and how it is harder for a black man to get back on his feet. I am not a black man. I am a black woman. But, I know that no matter how many applications I had to submit in a day or how many interviews I had to take, or how far I had to drive to get to them, I would have done it endlessly, because my kids need a roof over their head, food to eat, electricity, and running water. Facts are facts. You just gotta make things happen, no matter what.

Being that Philly had one son, you would think he thought the same way as me. But, he did not. And unfortunately, I am still the kind of woman that is going to help someone in need, even if it puts me in a bind.

He did try for a company that was equal to what he had done, and he really did well on the interview. Philly even got a second interview, but they did not choose him in the end. That was very disheartening, and I could see he felt helpless and overwhelmed to have gotten so far in the process, just to not be selected and never know why.

On the downside, I was still not married. Engaged twice officially but never married. Philly was having so many ups and downs, but while on the upside, I became pregnant again. This was mind-blowing news because I knew I wanted to be married before I had another child. I had never been married before. But, still, it was joyous for me.

"I'm pregnant," I told Philly excited.
"I'm not in no situation right now to have no baby," he told me. We did not talk for a week after this.

Why does a man have sex with a woman and then freeze when he finds out she is pregnant? What did he think would happen? Even both of the boys' Dads were happy. But Philly just could not get out of his mindset. I prayed to God on what to do because I knew that if I had this child, everything would be on me. "I do not want to be made a single mother again by yet another man, but I also do not want to have an abortion," I prayed, as I spoke to God for guidance. Philly stayed secluded, not answering my phone calls.

Then, I had a gut-wrenching dream. It started out that I was in a prison and, in the beginning of the dream, I thought I worked there as a nurse. But I soon realized I had on an orange jumpsuit and that I was actually a prisoner. I did not know what crime I had committed. I called my sister, Rochelle, from the prison and told her I needed help. I told her that I got a letter and that they said they were going to execute me. She told me that it had to be a mistake, but that she's really, really busy writing a paper for her doctorate, and for me just to call them and tell them it was a mistake. I kept telling her that I really needed her to help me because no one was listening to me and I did not know why I was in here. She told me to hold on, and she made a phone call. When she came back on the line, she told me that they were going to give me a meeting in an hour and that I needed to show up at the meeting.

As I entered the room for the meeting, there was a round table with men and women around the table in business attire, more than seven people in attendance. There was a lady reading from a paper. "You're going to be executed today. There is nothing you can say," she said. She never told me what crime I was accused of, but then suddenly, she stopped talking and turned her attention to another woman entering the room with nursing scrubs on, holding a red tube of blood. "Because of what's in this tube, your life will be spared," said a man in a business suit. "We are going to give you another chance. We aren't going to execute you and we are going to let you go free because you have something special inside of you that needs to come out and impact the world and change lives. Don't take this warning lightly. You need to protect what's inside of you by all means."

I woke up in a panic. I sat straight up in the bed just breathing fast, trying to catch my breath. I was looking around my room calling on Jesus and then that is when it hit me that I was gonna have this baby and make sure it lived.

The next day, I had a hair appointment. My beautician told me that her pastor could interpret dreams, so she called her pastor and from what I told her, she told me what he thought. She told me that in the dream where I called my sister and she could not bail me out, but was able to get me a meeting, meant that, for whatever was coming up next in my life, my sister was not going be there like she used to be. So, I would have to ask and trust

God for the next journey of my life like I had never done before. Then, she went on to say that the tube of blood represented something inside of me, maybe a baby, but more of a gift that had to be shared with the world and that the gift from God was in my womb. The gift had to grow, and I was in charge of protecting it and making sure only good things were around me and going inside of me. The gift would touch so many lives.

The last part of the dream, she said, that when I was given a second chance and warned not to take it lightly, it meant that if I reject this gift, God would shut up my womb and give the gift to someone else, because God wanted this gift to come into the world regardless.

"I do not know if you are pregnant," she said. "And, I do not know whether the gift is a child or if it is just a story you have to share that will help others, but I know you have some kind of gift and that you need to protect the gift as the person in the dream said."

Later that day, I went over to Philly's house and I kept knocking on the door until he answered, because I knew he was in there. This time, however, I was not leaving until we talked about me having this baby. He finally answered the door and we talked in the vestibule as soon as I walked in. I did not want to prolong the conversation any longer. I told him that I made the decision that I am going to have this baby. I would have told him about the dream that I had, but it would not have made a difference, because he just would not have seen it the same way. I told him that if I had to do it by myself, I would. I knew that it would all be on me, financially. He asked me again if I was sure and again, I said yes. Then, I closed my eyes and talked to God in my head and said to myself, 'God I am protecting this baby. You told me to protect this baby so please help me. I need your help right now.'

"I'm just going to ask you one more time and then after this I won't ever ask you again, but are you sure?" Philly asked.

"Yes, I am having this baby." Then, that was it and he didn't bring it up ever again!

I so wanted this baby to be a girl. I already had two boys and I just wanted a little girl so badly because I believe little girls just give you extra strength.

The day I found out, I had just gotten off from the night shift and I had only been asleep for about two hours when, of course, I had to get up and use the bathroom. As I looked at my phone, I saw that I had missed the phone call from the doctor, and I had given them permission to leave a voicemail with results. Do I listen to the voicemail and risk the chance that it is not the news I want to hear and then lie awake feeling sad? Or, do I listen to the voicemail and get the news I desire and be so excited that I cannot go back to sleep still anyway? I would not be able to go back to sleep knowing the answer is a button away. So, of course, I listened to the voicemail.

The nurse practitioner went all around the world talking about how I am negative for trisomy 21 and how I am negative for down syndrome and so on. Then finally she said, "You have only X chromosomes and no Y chromosomes so you're having a baby girl." I had drawn up a long prayer that I was going to pray once I heard the news, but all I could do now was get off my bed, get on my knees, and cry.

"Thank you, Jesus, Thank you Jesus," I kept praying to God and crying happy tears.

As with my second son, I did not immediately announce the pregnancy to family or friends because of the loss I once had. Day in and day out, I did not tell not one soul - not my immediate family, not my coworkers, and not my church. I wanted to make it over 24 weeks before telling anyone. At about 25 weeks, I was ready to tell everyone. My sister was having her housewarming party, and this was the first house that she ever owned in her name. But it was more of a get-together because she had lived in her own place before, just not with outright ownership. She had mentioned that she was going to move up the date of the housewarming, but I asked her if she could push it to a later date. I did not let my sister know that the reason why I was asking was because I wanted to wait until the ultrasound would be clearer for me to show her when I made the announcement. She agreed.

When I arrive for the housewarming, she and her husband had made Jello shots and I had to keep telling them, "Oh, not right now. I need to eat first." Everyone was celebrating, having a good time. I had a lot of family come down and two of my best friends were there - Carmen and Annette - that did not even know the secret.

I have known Carmen since I was five years old. She drove up from North Carolina just thinking she was coming for my sister's housewarming. Carmen and I even stayed at her hotel the night before to catch up and she had not even noticed anything about my body. Annette was living with me at that time and had not noticed anything either. My co-workers in labor and delivery, however, who I changed uniforms within the locker room, knew. It was hard to tell for most people because I carry really small, mostly gaining weight in my breasts and hips.

"I have a gift for you," I told my sister even though she had told everyone not to bring any gifts. She and I were standing in the center of her living room with everyone around us watching. My sister has always wanted a little girl. She had a son and that was her only child.

"I wish one of your boys had been a girl," my sister used to say years before.

Philly was there recording from my sister's phone and I had my nephew's girlfriend recording from my phone for two different angles of the announcement. My nephew's girlfriend did not know what the surprise was. She just knew to hold the phone. I set up a decoy and let my sister first open an envelope, as a gift from my sons, that was taped to one side of a gift bag. They were handmade coupons from my older son to give free vacuum cleaning and free leaf raking at her new house. Then, she read the other card from me, taped on the other side of the gift bag, and in it was a card giving her kudos for all her accomplishments.

"What do you give a woman who now has everything?" Rochelle read. "A fiancé? A car? Clothes? There is not anything you can buy her that she doesn't already have. Please save room for me in your new house, love."

And, then there was another envelope that she had to open. On the inside of the envelope, it said, "Your niece comes in February of next year." My sister still did not get it until she flipped the paper over and saw the ultrasound. She lost it! She threw the bag up in the air and starts screaming! My sister ran over to me and grabbed me up. She was jumping up and down and started pulling me around the room, but I was trying not to topple over and was bracing myself to protect my belly and we almost fell to the floor! The whole room was still confused.

"What is it?" some people shouted.

"It's one million dollars?!" my brother shouted randomly.

"No!" my sister yelled. "It's better than $1 million!"

"It's a baby!" my friend Carmen screamed once she saw the ultrasound picture on the floor. Then, Annette screamed in opera note.

"The hell it is!" my Mom said and proceeded to walk over to pick the ultrasound picture up off the floor to inspect it. Mom was still confused and just kept staring at it because she had thought I was done with having babies. My youngest was already ten years old.

"Did you know?!" Carmen turned to Annette and asked, since Annette had been living with me at the time. But Annette had no idea.

"Did you know?!" Carmen then turned to Philly and asked.

"Of course, he knew!" Annette answered for him.

But Philly did not want to make the announcement like this because, although my sister was ecstatic, he felt I was trying to take the attention off my sister's housewarming and put it on me. But I had to keep telling him that I know my sister, and this was actually a really good surprise for her. Once he saw her reaction, he understood.

"This was the best gift and I loved the whole surprise," she confirmed.

"That's why you didn't take the Jello shots!"

At work the next day, my co-workers threw me a little reveal party. Everyone was just so excited for me and I was thankful for their genuine happiness for me.

Everything was going well with the pregnancy until one day after work. I got home early in the morning at 8 a.m. as usual and went to sleep. When I woke up at 4 p.m., I started doing my daily routine as usual, straightening up and starting dinner for me and the boys. But, around 7 o'clock, I realized that I had not felt her move in my belly since I had been up. I immediately headed to the hospital, being a labor and delivery nurse and knowing all the bad signs. I tried to call Philly, but he was at his house dead asleep because he had worked overtime that day. So, I called my sister.

"I'll meet you at the hospital," Rochelle said.

Carmen was keeping me calm on speaker phone until I got to the hospital. I checked in at the ER desk, and then sat and waited for someone from labor and delivery to come get me. After sitting for five minutes, I panicked. I know how precious seconds are in this type of situation when an expecting mother is not feeling the baby, after she has been faithful with doing all the things that the doctors have told her to do over the course of the pregnancy.

The ER clerk saw the panic on my face and called up to labor and delivery, who said they were on their way down. My eyes started to well up with tears, and right before I began to cry, Carmen called my phone. She was able to keep me calm until the labor and delivery nurse came.

The nurse took a urine sample and then placed me in the hospital bed. All I wanted her to do was to put the monitor on me so that I could hear my baby 's heartbeat and it felt like forever before she did.
But there it was a nice, strong heartbeat. I was only 36 weeks pregnant, so her lungs were mature enough to be born, if need be, but I am glad she did not need to be born just yet. When my sister walked into the room, I had

only been on the monitor for three minutes. Thankfully, Philly finally came to the hospital. I was discharged home and still pregnant.

Exactly two weeks later was déjà vu. I got off work early in the morning, and then I woke up around 4 p.m. to do my usual routine. Around 7 p.m., I realized that my baby girl had not moved since I woke up, but this time I stayed calm. I called the doctor and the doctor told me to come in and that they would be waiting for me. I put my bags in the car. I finished cooking dinner. And, then I drove to the hospital. This time, I did not panic in the waiting room. When I arrived on the unit, Brandy, a nurse with whom I used to work with, was fussing at me because I had not come straight to L&D after I called. She immediately put me on the monitor and the heartbeat was just fine again although, this time, I was contracting every one or two minutes. Not painful contractions, but I felt them. There was an off and on tightening of my belly. Philly came to the hospital much faster this time.

"I do not feel comfortable sending you home with the way the baby looks on the monitor," the doctor said. She wanted to give me pain medication to see if the contractions would go away because they were not going away with the IV fluids.

"You can give me the pain meds and then I'll go home," I said.
"No. If I give you the pain meds, you will have to spend the night."

I wanted to just take the pain meds and go because it did not hurt a lot. I was just gonna go home and tough it out. But Philly said we were staying, getting the meds, and letting them continue to monitor me overnight. Once they gave me the pain meds through the IV, I fell out for the night.

"I've been checking the monitor while you were sleeping," the doctor said when I woke up in the morning. "I am going to consult with MFM (maternal fetal medicine) and I'll get back to you right after that. When she came back into my room, she gave me two choices.
I could either be induced or I could be signed out AMA - 'Against Medical Advice.'

"I'm not comfortable with the way the baby has been looking on the monitor throughout the night," the doctor repeats.
"We're staying," Philly interjects, of course, before I even get a chance to say anything.

My sister had just left the hospital 15 minutes prior to the doctor showing up to talk to us. So, I immediately call my sister to come back because they are going to deliver me today. Rochelle quickly makes a U-turn and calls her employees to tell them she would not be in today. There was no way my sister was missing another delivery - especially for her niece.

They induced me with a medication called Pitocin that goes through the IV and it was making me contract strongly, but I still was not in pain. The doctor wanted to break my water, but I had my own knowledge as a labor and delivery nurse and insisted that it was too early. Still, about 45 minutes before the hospital shift change, the doctor comes in and breaks my water. Of course, two minutes later, the baby's heart rate goes down, but I knew what maneuvers I had to do to get the heart rate back up. All my L&D skills was kicking in.

"You are seven centimeters," my nurse told me.
"I'm ready for an epidural," I wasn't going to miss this time.

But, after the epidural, the baby's heart rate was still going down. I suddenly had a hard contraction and was ready to push, and indeed pushed her out in seven minutes with the umbilical cord wrapped around her neck. That was the problem all along. The doctor removed the umbilical cord from around her neck, once her head was out. They put her on my stomach, but she was not breathing, moving, or crying. The L&D nurse mode kicked in yet again and I started stimulating her by rubbing her back very vigorously.

"Did you call NICU, yet?" I questioned. I know I was the patient, but this was my child, so I was not going to be stopped from doing what I know I had to do.

My sister was trying to take videos with her new phone, and they told her she can only take pictures. But, unbeknownst to her, her new phone could take pictures and videos at the same time. So, we were able to keep the best moment on video when my baby gave her first cry and first breath. She started to move around, and they took her over to the NICU nurses to be checked on. This little lady was born through adversity already. I know she'll do well in life, no matter what comes her way!!!

I was sitting in my postpartum room holding her, and just staring at her and kissing her chubby cheeks when my cellphone rings. She had not even been born for 14 hours and already one of Philly's creditors was calling me. I put the creditor on loudspeaker for Philly to hear and I just looked at him.

"This is the LAST time I am helping you financially," I said next. At that moment, I had to make a choice, and I chose my daughter. I did not want my daughter to grow up thinking that she should financially take care of a man who could not take care of her, or for her to be in a bind because she was helping other people, while she was going without. I wanted to be able to show her how to be free from financial adversity and be able to take that freedom and help others.

Up until this point, I had been loaning Philly money to help him stay afloat, but in the process, I was accruing a whole bunch of credit card debt. I lent it to him because I felt that if you are with someone, you should have their back and help them when times get rough. The only problem was that this was not a short time period that I was helping him. It had been going on for a whole year and two months!

I was a single mother of two kids. Philly and I were not married. No vows had been exchanged before God and so taking care of Philly should have never been a part of my vocabulary.

Have you ever had to carry all the weight on your shoulders and make sure all the bills are paid and that the kids are taken care of?

Then, on top of that, you have a very intense job where critical seconds count all day long, making the difference between a life being saved or a life being lost?

Or, have you ever had a job where your supervisors were gunning for you and wanted to fire you just because they do not like you for some personal reason?

Are you dealing with work and then taking care of a household?

This was my life and I would not allow my daughter to have any taste of it. I wanted her to grow up and believe she could be the CEO of her own business. I had to get my way of life in order and be the right example for her to copy. Kids mimic your every move when they are growing up - the way you talk, laugh, how you handle struggles, and how you treat people around you. I want her to imitate my strengths. I cannot teach my boys how to be a man. I can teach them about God, how to treat women, and to be respectful, to start. But I have definitely been through enough to be able to teach this little lady how to be a strong woman, on top of everything else.

After my Blessing turned nine months old, her father wanted to move in. Philly said he wanted to have both of his children under one roof. I did not want him to move in because I said the next man that I live with needs to be my husband. However, and you are going to be mad about this, I did let him move in. But this was because there were other surrounding circumstances. I told him that things needed to be in order within a year. Philly agreed to this, but in a year thing were worse.

I was still a night shift nurse and had been for years even before meeting Philly. He was again depressed and very irritable. He constantly wanted to argue at the wrong time. You know how your Mom used to say, 'there's a time and a place for everything?' Well, I do not think he paid attention to that lesson.

After working a 12-hour night shift, I would get home in the morning and he would see me come in through the door, but not say one word to me. There was not a 'good morning,' not a 'hello,' not a 'how was your night?' Nothing. I would shower, get in the bed, and then two hours later he would come in and wake me up to argue over some petty stuff that could have waited.

Why couldn't he have waited until I woke up or until I walked in the door? I actually had to try to explain to him that I am in control of people's lives at work and that sleep was important for me to do my job well. I had to explain that when he disturbs my sleep for all these little things, he put my career, and our well-being in jeopardy.

He ignored this every time. So, I had to start taking drastic measures. I would literally come home, get my daughter dressed for school, take her to school, and then go over to my father's house or my friend's house and go to sleep until it was time to pick my daughter up from daycare. This was the only way I could keep my career safe, which provided for all of us. I hated having to go this far.

Philly would even have inappropriate conversations with my oldest son, telling him things like, "You know your Mom has another boyfriend, right? That's why she doesn't come home."

When I found out, I had to check him on it immediately. I don't involve children into adult business like that, even if it's true. Children are not your equal. Philly tried to pretend that he was just playing when he told my son those things. But I knew better. He was trying to demean my character to my own children. And, like I said, I am an adult. I do not cheat. If I do not want to be with someone, I can just let them know that I do not want to be with them. There's no need for me to cheat in a relationship. I am all-in, one hundred and twenty percent. It was wrong for him to try to taint my image to my son, just because things between us were not working out, and because he did not know how to do what he needed to do.

"We can talk about this later, not in front of the kids," I would have to say to him calmly without getting into it right then and there. It was getting to the point where Philly would just start arguing and yelling, and he did not care that the kids were around. I purposely would not respond to his provocations. But he would just go on and on and be loud in the process.

When Philly started yelling at me in front of the kids and getting so comfortable with this bad habit, I knew this relationship was not going to get better. My kids were not going to grow up thinking this was normal. I resorted to writing him a letter. I let Philly know my expectations - that the boys needed to be kept up with in terms of their grades and their chores, and that Philly needed to help around the house more and share a certain amount of the bills.

"This is an ultimatum. I'm not doing it," Philly resisted as soon as he finished reading.

"This is not an ultimatum," I said, picking up the letter and reading through it again. "I'm not telling you that we need to get married tomorrow. I am pleading for your help around the house. I am pleading for your help with these bills. I got all this weight, all these struggles on my shoulders to carry alone and, if we're in a relationship, I shouldn't be carrying all of this by myself".

"All right. I'll do it," Philly came to me the next day and agreed. But a week went by and he still was not doing anything I asked in the letter. He switched up.

"Yeah, I'm not going to be able to do this," he said.
"Okay, well then we just need to call it. We need to go our separate ways and maybe do what we need to do apart. Maybe later down the road we can get back together when some things have been fixed", I said, remaining firm.

I did everything that I could do here. You cannot help somebody who does not have it inside of himself to help himself. He had no push, no drive, no fight to take back control of his life. There was nothing in him to save the relationship and be a provider. I did not sign up for this. I was not going to make things any harder for myself or for my children. If you cannot save yourself, how can you save someone else? I love helping people, but if I am not in the right mindset, the right financial situation, or do not have the strength, then I cannot help you either.

Despite all that I have been through with other men in the past, this was the worst breakup. What I mean by that, is that when I broke up with the others, it was understood that we were not going to be together anymore because of what they did - the cheating or the beating. But, in Philly's illogical way of thinking, all he could see was that I was putting him out. He and his other child.

"This is not unconditional love," he would say. But I know I deserve a man who shows up for me. I know my worth. I had all these little eyes looking at me, seeing what I was going to do. It did not mean I do not know how to love unconditionally. It means I know how to love me, and that I am willing to love myself more than a person who has no standards, in times of adversity. My daughter must know that there are standards for any relationship.

I sacrificed a lot being in that relationship with Philly. Before I met him, I used to go on three vacations a year - twice with the girls and once with the kids. But I sacrificed all that to tighten up my financial responsibilities. After the breakup with Philly, I got right back to my vacations, after seven months. All the immediate peace I had in my life once he was gone, you don't how good it felt. No more sleepless days. No more arguing. No more trying to fix all a grown man's problems and still getting lashed out on. No more complaining. No more negativity in my environment. Do you know what it feels like to have peace back in your life when you have not had it in a long time? I know Philly has it in him to get back to where he used to be. Out of all my children's fathers, he spends the most time with our daughter. He would die for her, but I want him to live for her.

As far as co-parenting, things were not going well. Philly was not giving me anything financially to help with his daughter. He kept making excuses, but I was ready for it by this point because VA did the same thing. See, they know they did not do what they were supposed to do, but still resented me for breaking up with them. They resented me for not being the person they could mistreat, because they were being mistreated out in the world, and needed someone controllable to take revenge on. They resented me for knowing my worth and taking a stand. But, guess what? I'll take that resentment in exchange for my peace. I'll take that resentment in exchange for my daughter having the chance to know her worth. I'll take that resentment for my sons knowing how to value any woman in their lives.

CHAPTER 7
PERSEVERANCE EQUALS WINNING

All these relationships put me into $70,000 worth of debt and took my credit score down from 780 to 555. If you are in a similar situation, boy do I have advice for you. A lot of advice, in fact, which I plan on sharing with you soon.

I should have broken up with Queens the second time he did not come home. I would just listen to his excuses, that he had too much to drink and he fell asleep over at his boy's house, and that's why the sun beat him home. Every woman has that gut feeling, that woman's intuition, and sometimes we choose to see only the good in a person and ignore all the red flags waving in our face.

I should have broken up with Country Boy after he hit me the first time. I should have never let him sweet talk me back. Abusive men always promise that they 'won't do it again' and when they do it again, they make you believe it is your fault that you were hit. They make you believe the only reason why they hit you is because they love you and are scared of the thought of you not being with them. A real man would never put his hands on a woman. I am thankful that I was able to get out of that abusive relationship alive.

I should have broken up with VA once I knew he lied about not being separated. Instead I was just thinking, 'I don't want to raise this child by myself'. Little did I know that being in a relationship and being cheated on was way more stressful than being a single mother of two kids. Even with concrete proof that he was cheating, I still could not bring myself to break up with him. So, I literally broke down over the kitchen table crying, and started praying to God to help me because I could not do it myself. My prayer gave me the strength to put all his things in those trash bags and break up with him.

I should have broken up with Philly once I realized that he would never pay me back all the money I kept lending him, especially with him never having a steady job. I just dug a deeper and deeper hole for myself while I was helping him to get out of the deep hole he was already in. I figured that you should help the person you love, no matter what, because these kinds of situations happen from time to time, and your man will pay you back eventually. That is what I would want someone to think of and do for me if I needed serious help for a while.

I also should have never lived with a man that I was not married to. This would have saved me from exposing my kids to all the unhealthy arguments, seeing their Mom so physically and mentally exhausted. I wholeheartedly apologize that I interrupted my boys' lifestyle of vacationing and having fun. That was our special time every year, at the end of the school year. I assured them I will never let any of that happen again.

I had to have a strong mindset to persevere through my relationships. I definitely had to ask for help from God through it all. I envisioned reciprocity from these relationships, which I never received. But, when I was finally able to see that they were incapable of it, I ended the relationships. When you get your mind set on how you are supposed to be treated, how you are supposed to be loved, then it only makes sense to part ways with someone when all efforts have been exhausted. Having the right mindset can make your decisions much easier to make.

A lot of people do not realize how important vacation is throughout these kinds of difficult times. They see vacation just as a luxury, when it is actually a necessity in today's society. Today's society has so many single parent homes, or homes where family time is not the centerpiece of the home life as it used to be. Things are way more expensive now, and a lot of single parents are working two jobs just to keep a roof over their heads. So, there is no time to spend true quality time with family. Then, if you are a couple, and one person is not working then the other person is either working a second job, or putting in overtime just to make ends meet for the both of you, this continuous cycle, with no breaks in between, is detrimental to the health of our minds. All-inclusive vacations are where it's at.

But, first, an adult vacation is always needed. Maybe a girls' trip or a guys' trip if you are single. If you are married, then a couples' trip. Then, a family trip with the kids would be next. I say all-inclusive for families because you want everything to already be taken care of. Choose a resort that has 24-hour, room service or something open for the whole time so that you can choose when you wanna wake up and when you wanna go lay out on the beach.

For me, the beach is just so serene, and just to hear the ocean and the waves hit up against the shore is healing. Sometimes, we do not even realize how much rest we lose while dealing with every stressor in our lives. We put our bodies under so much stress when we are always on the go. Whatever you prefer, find your peaceful and positive way of resetting and make sure you do it as often as you need to. We need to reset our minds for every new stage in our journey of life. This is a great way to give yourself a renewed mindset.

Some people grow up being told that they cannot do something or that they cannot achieve the things they want to achieve in life. You will never be someone if you start to believe them and say those same things to yourself. You might have been put down. You might have grown up around a lot of chaos or you might have been in a lot of chaotic relationships. Your mindset might be consumed with negativity. But, remember the age-old saying that 'hurt people, hurt people.' Now that you are an adult, you are in charge of your environment, and whatever you do not like, you need to change it. You are not a child anymore. You control your friends and who you are around in your off time.

Reading books and articles that inspire you, or anything that helps educate you, renews your mindset, too. Seek out information that is going to help you to further any goals you have set for yourself. It is never too late to start your own business. I can point you in the right direction, too.

I did not know where to begin, but what I did know is that I did not want to work for someone else the rest of my life. I did not like when I had supervisors or bosses that brought so much chaos and hostility to my work environment. I had to deal with favoritism, cliques, unprofessionalism, rudeness, supervisors picking on certain employees, and the list keeps on going.

Have you ever had any of that on your job? That is why if you create your own business, you can be the supervisor you never had - treat people fairly or treat people with the dignity and the respect that you have always wanted in a work relationship. Create a family out of your work environment. I also want my children to have their own business in order, to provide a tradition that can be passed down from generation to generation. Even if it has never been done in my family, I am okay with being the first in any positive endeavor! Are you okay with being the first in your family??

I want my daughter to be with someone as powerful as her - a power couple. I want her to be with a man who supports her visions and dreams, a man who will be more than happy to help her achieve whatever positive goals she has in life.

I want my sons to grow up seeing me in a loving relationship. I do not want them to think that hitting a woman is love. If my sons ever started to get used to the violent chaos, they would have grown up to repeat the cycle or grow up to resent me for not leaving and protecting them. Now, don't get me wrong. In some abusive relationships, it is not so simple as saying 'it's over.' Sometimes, you literally need an escape plan. Not all abusers will just let you break up with them and walk out. You need to carefully assess your situation and the best way to do it. But there are always ways to get out safely with your kids in a quick fashion.

I know my spiritual foundation is why I am able to persevere. My strength perseveres because I rely on God. I have learned how to change my environment and rid myself of bad relationships and other habits. I have a savings account, emergency fund, and I now invest—
I have taken back my finances. I have paid over $30,000 of debt, that was not even my debt, but the debt I incurred from helping others. And, they never paid me back for this. I will not EVER keep lending money to people who never pay me back. I also only lend a certain amount. Anything past that, I say no.

An eye opener for me was staying with these men even in their darkest days and at their lowest points. Even though I was down in the trenches with them, I was not appreciated. Even though I lent them money, they never saw fit to pay it back, especially when we were no longer together. They could not see that this just takes away from their kids. I am thankful that God led me to a career in nursing where there is such a great demand for people with my skill set - where I could keep our lives afloat. I am ecstatic that I was NOT broken. I never left a relationship bitter and I always took the time to heal before even thinking about another relationship. When I tell you there is nothing better than having PEACE in your house, there is nothing like it.

There is no need to let someone take you out of your character. Always handle your business and never be provoked to do wrong. Take control of your actions because that is all you are in control of. Remove yourself from toxic people and environments. Elevate your mind and always look at the glass half full. Learn the lessons in both good and bad experiences. Never give up. There is always a plan B, C, and D through Z! Don't ever think you are the only one going through what you are going through and know there are people who have gotten through the same situation or worse. Find that person or group, and mimic that.

I have a special place in my heart for single Moms pushing through adversity and the hardships of raising their kids on their own - emotionally, physically, and financially. This link here is a place where anyone can donate to help these mothers, one family at a time. Donate here - UnstoppableNicole.com - and at the same website, I am also offering an online course for those ready to shift forward.

In whatever order you need this to happen. Or, just the ones you have lost control over, regaining control is the key to your success. Everyone is at different stages of their lives and they need to start seeking out the support they need now. There are ways to reclaim all of these. Would you like to learn from a Perseverance Expert who can help you reclaim any of these things in your life? You are not alone. Life can sometimes be rough for you or your loved ones that you support. This is okay, as long as you do not give up on yourself.

My motto is: "Giving up is Not an Option!" I help people dig themselves out of severe adversity. Who do you know, that is ready to TAKE IT BACK?

ABOUT THE AUTHOR

Nicole was born and raised in New York City
in Manhattan (Spanish Harlem).

It is when Nicole began teaching "teenage Bible Study" at
her church did she realize speaking was her true passion
and calling from God. She then served in a different
capacity and started a ministry called 4G (Four Women of
God). These four ladies would combine their money
together to buy food and go fellowship and serve food and
snacks to the members of the church while they were
rehearsing or working their ministry. Three of the four
ladies
were single Mothers including Nicole.

Nicole has created The Single Mom Perseverance Fund to
provide for single mothers so they can receive help to
include, but not limited to, covering groceries, monthly
rent/mortgage, utilities, daycare fees, pampers, children's
clothes and more by having sponsors that come in any
form (other single moms, organizations, people who were
raised by single moms etc...) to donate.

Nicole's passion is to speak and make an impact by creating
an awareness to bridge a gap for single mothers in areas
they lack, therefore being the best them and not stressed
out so they can focus on creating memories with their
children and teaching their kids and the next generations to
be wealthy in health, mindset and finances.

65621242R00070

Made in the USA
Middletown, DE
03 September 2019